Crochet Wraps
Every Which Way

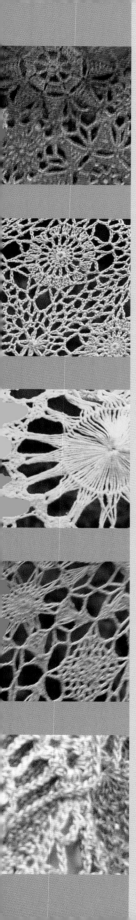

Crochet Wraps Every Which Way

18 Original Patterns in 6 Techniques

Tammy Hildebrand

STACKPOLE
BOOKS

Published by
STACKPOLE BOOKS
5067 Ritter Road
Mechanicsburg, PA 17055
www.stackpolebooks.com

Printed in U.S.A.

10 9 8 7 6 5 4 3 2 1

First edition

Cover design by Tessa J. Sweigert

Library of Congress Cataloging-in-Publication Data

Hildebrand, Tammy.
    Crochet wraps every which way : 18 original patterns in 6 techniques /
Tammy Hildebrand. — First edition.
       pages   cm
    Includes index.
    ISBN 978-0-8117-1183-8
    1. Crocheting—Patterns. 2. Shawls. I. Title.
TT825.H534 2014
746.43'4041—dc23
                                                        2013035331

Contents

Introduction

Is there anything more versatile than a wrap? One of the most long-lived garment designs in existence, a wrap can be anything from a light, lacy shawlette, to a thick, cozy poncho, to a huge, intricate, jaw-droppingly gorgeous lace shawl. No matter the season or the occasion—from formal to casual—there is a wrap or shawl out there that will suit perfectly. Many designs can be worn in multiple ways: wrapped around the neck to create a cowl, draped over one shoulder, draped over both shoulders, tied at the waist. Some would even make fabulous tablecloths!

Similarly, wraps can be made using a number of different techniques—which makes them great projects for learning and practicing new stitches and styles of crocheting! This book uses six different techniques that produce beautiful, unique results: traditional crochet, motifs, hairpin lace, broomstick lace, Tunisian crochet, and double-ended crochet. For each technique, three patterns are included, generally corresponding to a beginner project, an intermediate project, and an experienced project.

It is my hope that you will approach this book full of confidence and excitement to learn and experience new things. I am not a big fan of skill levels as they may intimidate some crocheters and put them off of trying something new. An "intermediate" or "experienced" pattern is nothing more than what you have already accomplished with easy patterns; you might just have to pay a little more attention. Maybe you will need to count stitches more frequently or use stitch markers. Perhaps there will be a stitch or technique that you will need to watch an online video of or practice a few times to become comfortable and familiar with. But you can do it!

It is best to first become proficient with basic stitches: chain, single crochet, half double crochet, double crochet, treble crochet, and slip stitch. Once you've mastered this handful of stitches, you'll be able to create anything you wish. The possibilities are endless! The old adage "practice makes perfect" really is true. Practice what you have learned until you feel confident to move on.

If you are already an accomplished crocheter, not to fear! I have included a number of designs that are sure to challenge. I have been crocheting for 40 years and designing for 17 years but I am still always learning. I have included designs in both hairpin lace and broomstick lace that are worked in the round. Using the techniques this way was a new experience for me, and once I started, I didn't want to stop. There are so many possibilities!

Have fun, experiment. Don't become discouraged and give up. Crocheting is supposed to be enjoyable, but that doesn't mean there might not be moments when it is frustrating. That can sometimes happen when learning anything new. Trust me, the effort will be worth it.

I hope that my book will be a wonderful starting point for you to expand your horizons and reach for new goals. Enjoy!

Tips and Hints

1. If you wish to achieve the exact measurements a pattern calls for, you must first swatch. A swatch is a small sample of the stitch pattern. The hook size you use isn't so important; use whichever size hook that gives you the closest measurements to the gauge.

2. Have you ever eaten a cupcake before it was frosted because you just couldn't wait? It was probably good, but not as good as it could have been. Blocking is the same thing to crochet as frosting is to cupcakes. It is the finishing touch. The polish. I block just about everything I make and I love watching a design come to life.

3. Don't be afraid to stray from the pattern once you are confident. This is your project to create as you wish. Make it larger, make it smaller, maybe a different color—whatever brings you joy. Go for it!

4. I am a very visual learner. I love how there are many online videos now that make it so simple to learn new things. Grab a hook and your yarn to stitch along with a tutorial; it might be all you need to clarify what seems complicated in written word only.

5. Take the time to check your work as you go along. It is so sad to be halfway through a pattern and realize you made a mistake on your second row. I like to lay my piece out every couple of rows or rounds and just give it a quick "once-over."

6. If you do find a mistake, take the time to correct it. It is a difficult thing to tear out hours of work but if that is what it takes, put the effort in to perfect your project. It will be worth it in the end.

7. Always leave about a 4-inch length of yarn when fastening off. Using a yarn needle, weave your ends in securely, going back and forth in opposite directions. Knotting off yarn can leave unsightly bumps, and the knots can come untied. If you weave in your ends instead, you won't have to risk this happening and the ends will be invisible for a more polished finish.

8. If you just can't figure something out in a pattern, set it down for a few days and then come back to it to see if it makes sense after a break. Sometimes that's all it takes.

9. These particular designs are done in some of my favorite colors. Your projects need to be done in *your* favorite colors. Don't be afraid to switch things up!

10. Have fun! That is the most important advice I can give you. Crocheting should be a joy for you to do. No stressing, just enjoyment!

Abbreviations

Beg	begin/beginning
Ch	chain
Ch-sp	chain space
Cm	centimeter(s)
Dc	double crochet
Hdc	half double crochet
Rnd(s)	round(s)
RS	right side
Sc	single crochet
Sl st	slip stitch
Sp(s)	space(s)
St(s)	stitch(es)
Tr	treble crochet
Yd(s)	yard(s)
Yo	yarn over
*	repeat instructions following asterisk as directed
( )	work stitches in same st or sp
[ ]	work bracketed instructions specified number of times

Traditional Crochet

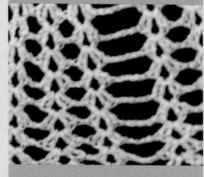

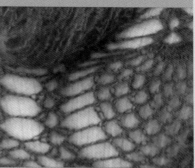

Crochet is the art of using a hook to create fabric from yarn or thread by pulling loops of the fiber through other loops. No one is quite sure where or when it originated since there are no known records of the craft prior to 1800. In its early days, crochet was a pastime of the upper class, who created detailed pieces to decorate their homes and adorn their clothing. The lower class was discouraged from crochet, as they didn't need these luxuries, and instead encouraged to knit necessities such as socks and housewares. During the Great Irish Famine (from 1845 to 1849), Ursuline nuns taught local women and children to crochet. Their creations, which we know today as Irish lace, were shipped to America and Europe to sell. The upper class labeled this as cheap imitation lace and shunned crochet. It wasn't until Queen Victoria learned to crochet that some of the stigma against the craft was lifted. The twentieth century saw patterns becoming readily available, with standardized stitch abbreviations and hook sizes coming into use.

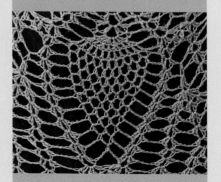

A virtual crochet renaissance began in 2004, as crocheters began using the internet to connect with other crocheters around the world. Crochet forums and email lists/groups made it easy for crocheters to share photos of their projects with each other. Designers and publishers began to make more and more crochet patterns available for purchase and download online as well. Crocheters can now use a number of websites to find new pattern ideas, research yarn options, and even connect with their favorite crochet designers. This online crochet renaissance resulted in an explosion in the popularity of crochet, making crochet more exciting, fun, and innovative today than it has ever been.

All crochet projects, even widely varying ones, are based on the same basic stitches—single crochet, double crochet, slip stitch, and so on. To learn how to make these stitches, or for a refresher, please see the step-by-step instructions starting on page 76.

Aqua Marine

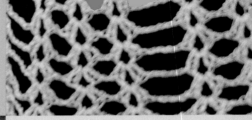

SKILL LEVEL

EASY

This sassy little shawl would add a little extra color worn over a prom dress or a bridesmaid's gown. Made in white, it would add just the right touch for a special bride. If you're looking for something a bit more casual, try it in a cotton-blend or acrylic yarn.

FINISHED SIZE

65½ [73½] in./166.5 (186.5) cm around bottom,
12 in./30.5 cm long

Average size to fit up to 44 in./112 cm bust; plus size
to fit up to 52 in./132 cm bust

YARN

Berroco Captiva (60% Cotton, 23% Polyester,
17% Acrylic; 1.75 oz/50 g, 98 yd./90 m hank):
4 hanks #5512 Aqua

CROCHET HOOK

US J-10 (6 mm) or size needed to obtain gauge

ADDITIONAL MATERIALS

Yarn needle

Size ⅝ in. (16 mm) shank button

GAUGE

3 sh and 2 ch-1 sps in pattern = 4 in./10 cm;
6 rows = 4 in./10 cm

Special Stitches

Beg-sh (beginning shell): (Sl st, ch 3, dc, ch 2, 2 dc) in
indicated space.

Sh (shell): (2 dc, ch 2, 2 dc) in indicated space or stitch.

Instructions

NOTE Instructions as written are for average size
with changes for plus size in brackets.

Ch 60 [66].

Row 1: Dc in 4th ch from hook and in each ch across—
58 [64] dc.

Row 2: Ch 3 (counts as dc here and throughout), (dc,
ch 2, 2 dc) in same st, *sk next 2 sts, sh in next st;
repeat from * across—20 [22] sh.

Row 3: Ch 1, turn, sk first st, sl st in next st, beg-sh in
next ch-2 sp, *ch 1, sh in ch-2 sp of next sh; repeat
from * across—20 [22] sh, 19 [21] ch-1 sps.

Row 4: Ch 1, turn, sk first st, sl st in next st, beg-sh in
next ch-2 sp, *ch 2, sh in ch-2 sp of next sh; repeat
from * across—20 [22] sh, 19 [21] ch-2 sps.

Row 5: Ch 1, turn, sk first st, sl st in next st, beg-sh in
next ch-2 sp, *ch 3, sh in ch-2 sp of next sh; repeat
from * across—20 [22] sh, 19 [21] ch-3 sps.

Row 6: Ch 1, turn, sk first st, sl st in next st, beg-sh in
next ch-2 sp, *ch 4, sh in ch-2 sp of next sh; repeat
from * across—20 [22] sh, 19 [21] ch-4 sps.

Row 7: Ch 1, turn, sk first st, sl st in next st, beg-sh in
next ch-2 sp, *ch 5, sh in ch-2 sp of next sh; repeat
from * across—20 [22] sh, 19 [21] ch-5 sps.

Row 8: Ch 1, turn, sk first st, sl st in next st, beg-sh in
next ch-2 sp, ch 5, sh in ch-2 sp of next sh, *sh in
center ch of next ch-5 sp, sh in ch-2 sp of next sh,
ch 5, sh in ch-2 sp of next sh; repeat from * across—
29 [32] sh, 10 [11] ch-5 sps.

Row 9: Ch 1, turn, sk first st, sl st in next st, beg-sh in next ch-2 sp, ch 5, *sh in ch-2 sp of next 3 sh, ch 5; repeat from * 8 [9] more times, sh in ch-2 sp of last sh.

Rows 10–17: Ch 1, turn, sk first st, sl st in next st, beg-sh in next ch-2 sp, ch 5, *[sh in ch-2 sp of next sh, ch 1] 2 times, sh in ch-2 sp of next sh, ch 5; repeat from * 8 [9] more times, sh in ch-2 sp of last sh—29 [32] sh, 10 [11] ch-5 sps, 18 [20] ch-1 sps.

Finishing

With a yarn needle, weave in ends. Immerse the piece in cool water, then squeeze out the excess water, taking care not to wring or twist. Place the piece on a towel on a flat surface and gently stretch to open up the lace pattern. Leave until completely dry.

Purple Passion

SKILL LEVEL

INTERMEDIATE

Wispy and light, this wrap is like wearing a weightless cloud. The repetitive stitch pattern makes it a nice, relaxing project once you get going. The pattern is written with two repeats, but you can stop at one pattern repeat for a narrow, scarf version or add an additional repeat for a wider shawl.

FINISHED SIZE

16 in./40.5 cm wide by 60 in./152.5 cm long

YARN

Lion Brand LB Collection Silk Mohair (70% Super Kid Mohair, 30% Silk); 0.88 oz/25 g, 231 yd./212 m ball):

6 balls #147 Iris

CROCHET HOOK

US G-6 (4 mm) or size needed to obtain gauge

ADDITIONAL MATERIALS

Yarn needle

GAUGE

2 shells and one pineapple at widest point = 8 in./20.5 cm; Rows 1–8 = 4 in./10 cm

Special Stitches

Beg-sh (Beginning shell): (Sl st, ch 3, dc, ch 2, 2 dc) in indicated space.

Fsc (Foundation single crochet): This technique creates a foundation chain and a row of single crochet stitches in one.

Step 1: Place a slip knot on hook, ch 2, insert hook in 2nd ch from hook and draw up a loop; yarn over and draw through one loop on hook (the "chain"); yarn over and draw through 2 loops on hook (the "single crochet").

Step 2: Insert hook into the "chain" of the previous stitch and draw up a loop, yarn over and draw through one loop on hook (the "chain"), yarn over and draw through 2 loops on hook (the "single crochet"). Repeat for the length of foundation.

Sh (Shell): (2 dc, ch 2, 2 dc) in indicated space or stitch.

Instructions

Foundation Row: Work 209 Fsc.

Row 1: Ch 3 (counts as dc), (dc, ch 2, 2 dc) in first st, [ch 3, sk next 3 sts, sh in next st] twice, *[ch 3, sk next 3 sts, sc in next st] 7 times, [ch 3, sk next 3 sts, sh in next st] 3 times; repeat from * across—5 pattern repeats.

Row 2: Ch 1, turn, sk first st, sl st in next st, beg-sh in first ch-2 sp, [ch 3, sh in next ch-2 sp] twice, *ch 3, sk next ch-3 sp, [sc in next ch-3 sp, ch 3] 6 times, sk next ch-3 sp, sh in next ch-2 sp, [ch 3, sh in next ch-2 sp] twice; repeat from * across.

Row 3: Ch 1, turn, sk first st, sl st in next st, beg-sh in first ch-2 sp,[ch 3, sh in next ch-2 sp] twice, *ch 3, sk next ch-3 sp, [sc in next ch-3 sp, ch 3] 5 times, sk next ch-3 sp, sh in next ch-2 sp, [ch 3, sh in next ch-2 sp] twice; repeat from * across.

Row 4: Ch 1, turn, sk first st, sl st in next st, beg-sh in first ch-2 sp, ch 3, 10 dc in next ch-2 sp, ch 3, sh in next ch-2 sp, *ch 3, sk next ch-3 sp, [sc in next ch-3 sp, ch 3] 4 times, sk next ch-3 sp, sh in next ch-2 sp, ch 3, 10 dc in next ch-2 sp, ch 3, sh in next ch-2 sp; repeat from * across.

Row 5: Ch 1, turn, sk first st, sl st in next st, beg-sh in first ch-2 sp, ch 3, dc in next dc, [ch 1, dc in next dc] 9 times, ch 3, sh in next ch-2 sp, *ch 3, [sc in next ch-3 sp, ch 3] 3 times, sk next ch-3 sp, sh in next ch-2 sp, ch 3, dc in next dc, [ch 1, dc in next dc] 9 times, ch 3, sh in next ch-2 sp; repeat from * across.

Row 6: Ch 1, turn, sk first st, sl st in next st, beg-sh in first ch-2 sp, ch 3, [sc in next dc, ch 3] 10 times, sh in next ch-2 sp, *ch 3, sk next ch-3 sp, [sc in next ch-3 sp, ch 3] twice, sk next ch-3 sp, sh in next ch-2 sp, ch 3, [sc in next dc, ch 3] 10 times, sh in next ch-2 sp; repeat from * across.

Row 7: Ch 1, turn, sk first st, sl st in next st, beg-sh in first ch-2 sp, ch 3, sk next ch-3 sp, [sc in next ch-3 sp, ch 3] 9 times, sh in next ch-2 sp, *ch 3, sk next ch-3 sp, sh in next ch-3 sp, ch 3, sk next ch-3 sp, sh in next ch-2 sp, ch 3, sk next ch-3 sp, [sc in next ch-3 sp, ch 3] 9 times, sh in next ch-2 sp; repeat from * across.

Row 8: Ch 1, turn, sk first st, sl st in next st, beg-sh in first ch-2 sp, ch 3, sk next ch-3 sp, [sc in next ch-3 sp, ch 3] 8 times, sh in next ch-2 sp, *ch 3, [sh in next ch-2 sp, ch 3] twice, sk next ch-3 sp, [sc in next ch-3 sp, ch 3] 8 times, sh in next ch-2 sp; repeat from * across.

Row 9: Ch 1, turn, sk first st, sl st in next st, beg-sh in first ch-2 sp, ch 3, sk next ch-3 sp, [sc in next ch-3 sp, ch 3] 7 times, sh in next ch-2 sp, *ch 3, [sh in next ch-2 sp, ch 3] twice, sk next ch-3 sp, [sc in next ch-3 sp, ch 3] 7 times, sh in next ch-2 sp; repeat from * across.

Row 10: Ch 1, turn, sk first st, sl st in next st, beg-sh in first ch-2 sp, ch 3, sk next ch-3 sp, [sc in next ch-3 sp, ch 3] 6 times, sh in next ch-2 sp, *ch 3, [sh in next ch-2 sp, ch 3] twice, sk next ch-3 sp, [sc in next ch-3 sp, ch 3] 6 times, sh in next ch-2 sp; repeat from * across.

Row 11: Ch 1, turn, sk first st, sl st in next st, beg-sh in first ch-2 sp, ch 3, sk next ch-3 sp, [sc in next ch-3 sp, ch 3] 5 times, sh in next ch-2 sp, *ch 3, sc in next ch-3 sp, ch 3, sc in next ch-2 sp, ch 3, sc in next ch-3 sp, ch 3, sh in next ch-2 sp, ch 3, sk next ch-3 sp, [sc in next ch-3 sp, ch 3] 5 times, sh in next ch-2 sp; repeat from * across.

Row 12: Ch 1, turn, sk first st, sl st in next st, beg-sh in first ch-2 sp, ch 3, sk next ch-3 sp, [sc in next ch-3 sp, ch 3] 4 times, sh in next ch-2 sp, *ch 3, [sc in next ch-3 sp, ch 3] 4 times, sh in next ch-2 sp, ch 3, sk next ch-3 sp, [sc in next ch-3 sp, ch 3] 4 times, sh in next ch-2 sp; repeat from * across.

Row 13: Ch 1, turn, sk first st, sl st in next st, beg-sh in first ch-2 sp, ch 3, sk next ch-3 sp, [sc in next ch-3 sp, ch 3] 3 times, sh in next ch-2 sp, *ch 3, [sc in next ch-3 sp, ch 3] 5 times, sh in next ch-2 sp, ch 3, sk next ch-3 sp, [sc in next ch-3 sp, ch 3] 3 times, sh in next ch-2 sp; repeat from * across.

Row 14: Ch 1, turn, sk first st, sl st in next st, beg-sh in first ch-2 sp, ch 3, sk next ch-3 sp, [sc in next ch-3 sp, ch 3] twice, sh in next ch-2 sp, *ch 3, [sc in next ch-3 sp, ch 3] 6 times, sh in next ch-2 sp, ch 3, sk next ch-3 sp, [sc in next ch-3 sp, ch 3] twice, sh in next ch-2 sp; repeat from * across.

Row 15: Ch 1, turn, sk first st, sl st in next st, beg-sh in first ch-2 sp, ch 3, sk next ch-3 sp, sh in next ch-3 sp, ch 3, sh in next ch-2 sp, *ch 3, [sc in next ch-3 sp, ch 3] 7 times, sh in next ch-2 sp, ch 3, sh in next ch-3 sp, ch 3, sh in next ch-2 sp; repeat from * across.

Rows 16–28: Repeat Rows 2–14.

Finishing

With a yarn needle, weave in ends. Immerse the piece in cool water, then squeeze out the excess water, taking care not to wring or twist. Place the piece on a towel on a flat surface and gently stretch to open up the lace pattern. Leave until completely dry.

Perfect Pineapples

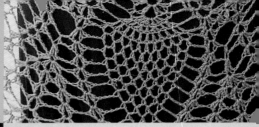

SKILL LEVEL

■■■□

EXPERIENCED

The pineapple has long been known as the symbol of welcome, friendship, and hospitality. Colonial Americans would honor guests by serving pineapples, which were rare and expensive. Through the years, the symbol of the pineapple began to appear in fine and decorative arts as well, including crochet. The pineapple was an incredibly popular motif in crochet patterns of the 1930s and 1940s. The easily recognizable shape, a wide base that dwindles to nothing at the tip, is still a motif beloved by crocheters and designers alike. This shawl is a beautiful blending of a very traditional symbol with the trendy circular shawl shape of today.

FINISHED SIZE

175 in./444.5 cm around; 55 in./139.5 cm across

YARN

Louet North America Euroflax Sport; (100% Wet Spun
Long Linen; 8 oz/227 g, 650 yd./594 m cone):
2 cones #37 Shamrock

CROCHET HOOK

US G-6 (4 mm) or size needed to obtain gauge

ADDITIONAL MATERIALS

Yarn needle

GAUGE

Rnds 1–3 = 4½ in./11.5 cm across

Special Stitches

Beg-sh (Beginning shell): (Sl st, ch 3, dc, ch 2, 2 dc) in
indicated space.

First-half-cl (First half of cluster): Keeping last loop of
each stitch on hook, 3 dc in indicated space (4 loops
remain on hook).

Second-half-cl (Second half of cluster): Keeping last
loop of each stitch on hook, 3 dc in next space, yarn
over and draw through all 7 loops on hook.

Sh (Shell): (2 dc, ch 2, 2 dc) in indicated space or stitch.

Instructions

Ch 4, join with sl st st to form ring.

Rnd 1: Ch 3 (counts as dc here and throughout), 15 dc
in ring, join with sl st st in top of beg-ch—16 dc.

Rnd 2: Ch 4 (counts as dc, ch 1 here and throughout),
*dc in next st, ch 1; repeat from * around, join with sl
st st in 3rd ch of beg ch-4—16 dc, 16 ch-1 sps.

Rnd 3: Sl st in next ch-1 sp, ch 1, sc in same sp, ch 1, (dc,
ch 3, dc) in next ch-1 sp, *ch 1, sc in next ch-1 sp, ch
1, (dc, ch 3, dc) in next ch-1 sp; repeat from * around,
ch 1, join with sl st st in beg-sc—8 sc, 16 dc, 8 ch-3
sps, 16 ch-1 sps.

Rnd 4: Sl st in each st to next ch-3 sp, sl st in same ch-3
sp, ch 6 (counts as dc, ch 3 here and throughout),
[dc, (ch 3, dc) twice] in same ch-3 sp, [dc, (ch 3, dc) 3
times] in each ch-3 sp around, join with sl st in 3rd ch
of beg ch-6—32 dc, 24 ch-3 sps.

Rnd 5: Sl st in first ch-3 sp, ch 1, sc in same sp, ch 1, 9 dc
in next ch-3 sp, ch 1, *(sc in next ch-3 sp, ch 1) twice,
9 dc in next ch-3 sp, ch 1; repeat from * around to
last ch-3 sp, sc in last ch-3 sp, ch 1, join with sl st in
beg-sc—16 sc, 72 dc, 24 ch-1 sps.

Rnd 6: Sl st in first ch-1 sp, sl st in next 3 sts, ch 1, sc in
same st, sc in next 4 sts, ch 2, sk next ch-1 sp, sh in
next ch-1 sp, ch 2, *sk next ch-1 sp, sk next 2 sts, sc in
next 5 sts, ch 2, sk next ch-1 sp, sh in next ch-1 sp, ch
2; repeat from * around, join with sl st in beg-sc—40
sc, 8 sh.

Rnd 7: Sl st in next st, ch 1, sc in same st, sc in next 2 sts,
ch 3, sk next ch-2 sp, sh in next ch-2 sp, ch 3, *sk next
ch-2 sp, sk next sc, sc in next 3 sts, ch 3, sk next ch-2
sp, sh in next ch-2 sp, ch 3; repeat from * around, join
with sl st in beg-sc—24 sc, 8 sh, 16 ch-3 sps.

Rnd 8: Sl st in next st, ch 1, sc in same st, ch 5, sk next
ch-3 sp, [2 dc, (ch 3, 2 dc) 3 times] in next ch-2 sp,
ch 5, sk next ch-3 sp, sk next sc, *sc in next st, ch 5, sk
next ch-3 sp, [2 dc, (ch 3, 2 dc) 3 times] in next ch-2
sp, ch 5, sk next ch-3 sp, sk next sc; repeat from *
around, join with sl st in beg-sc—8 sc, 64 dc, 16 ch-5
sps.

Rnd 9: Sl st in next 3 ch, ch 1, sc in same ch, sh in next
ch-3 sp, 7 dc in next ch-3 sp, sh in next ch-3 sp, sc in
next ch-5 sp, ch 3, *sc in next ch-5 sp, sh in next ch-3
sp, 7 dc in next ch-3 sp, sh in next ch-3 sp, sc in next
ch-5 sp, ch 3; repeat from * around, join with sl st in
beg-sc—16 sc, 56 dc (not including sts in shells), 16 sh.

Rnd 10: Sl st in each st to next ch-2 sp, beg-sh in same
sp, sk next 2 sts, 2 dc in next st, (dc in next st, 2 dc in
next st) 3 times, sh in next ch-2 sp, ch 1, sk next ch-3
sp, *sh in next ch-2 sp, sk next 2 sts, 2 dc in next st,
(dc in next st, 2 dc in next st) 3 times, sh in next ch-2
sp, ch 1, sk next ch-3 sp; repeat from * around, join
with sl st in top of first dc—88 dc (not including sts in
shells), 16 sh.

Rnd 11: Sl st in each st to next ch-2 sp, beg-sh in same
sp, sk next 2 sts, sc in next st, (ch 1, sc in next st) 10
times, *sh in next 2 ch-2 sps, sk next 2 sts, sc in next
st, (ch 1, sc in next st) 10 times; repeat from * around
to last ch-2 sp, sh in last ch-2 sp, join with sl st in top
of beg-ch—88 sc, 16 sh.

Rnd 12: Sl st in each st to next ch-2 sp, beg-sh in same sp, sk next ch-1 sp, sc in next ch-1 sp, (ch 3, sc in next ch-1 sp) 7 times, sh in next ch-2 sp, ch 1, *sh in next ch-2 sp, sk next ch-1 sp, sc in next ch-1 sp, (ch 3, sc in next ch-1 sp) 7 times, sh in next ch-2 sp, ch 1; repeat from * around, join with sl st in top of beg-ch—64 sc, 16 sh.

Rnd 13: Sl st in each st to next ch-2 sp, beg-sh in same sp, sc in next ch-3 sp, (ch 3, sc in next ch-3 sp) 6 times, sh in next ch-2 sp, ch 1, *sh in next ch-2 sp, sc in next ch-3 sp, (ch 3, sc in next ch-3 sp) 6 times, sh in next ch-2 sp, ch 1; repeat from * around, join with sl st in top of beg-ch—56 sc, 16 sh.

Rnd 14: Sl st in each st to next ch-2 sp, beg-sh in same sp, sc in next ch-3 sp, (ch 3, sc in next ch-3 sp) 5 times, sh in next ch-2 sp, ch 1, *sh in next ch-2 sp, sc in next ch-3 sp, (ch 3, sc in next ch-3 sp) 5 times, sh in next ch-2 sp, ch 1; repeat from * around, join with sl st in top of beg-ch—48 sc, 16 sh.

Rnd 15: Sl st in each st to next ch-2 sp, beg-sh in same sp, sc in next ch-3 sp, (ch 3, sc in next ch-3 sp) 4 times, sh in next ch-2 sp, ch 3, *sh in next ch-2 sp, sc in next ch-3 sp, (ch 3, sc in next ch-3 sp) 4 times, sh in next ch-2 sp, ch 3; repeat from * around, join with sl st in top of beg-ch—40 sc, 16 sh.

Rnd 16: Sl st in each st to next ch-2 sp, beg-sh in same sp, sc in next ch-3 sp, (ch 3, sc in next ch-3 sp) 3 times, sh in next ch-2 sp, ch 1, sh in next ch-3 sp, ch 1, *sh in next ch-2 sp, sc in next ch-3 sp, (ch 3, sc in next ch-3 sp) 3 times, sh in next ch-2 sp, ch 1, sh in next ch-3 sp, ch 1; repeat from * around, join with sl st in top of beg-ch—32 sc, 24 sh.

Rnd 17: Sl st in each st to next ch-2 sp, beg-sh in same sp, sc in next ch-3 sp, (ch 3, sc in next ch-3 sp) twice, sh in next ch-2 sp, ch 1, [2 dc, (ch 2, 2 dc) 3 times] in next ch-2 sp, ch 1, *sh in next ch-2 sp, sc in next ch-3 sp, (ch 3, sc in next ch-3 sp) twice, sh in next ch-2 sp, ch 1, [2 dc, (ch 2, 2 dc) 3 times] in next ch-2 sp, ch 1; repeat from * around, join with sl st in top of beg-ch—24 sc, 64 dc (not including sts in shells), 16 sh.

Rnd 18: Sl st in each st to next ch-2 sp, beg-sh in same sp, sc in next ch-3 sp, ch 3, sc in next ch-3 sp, sh in next ch-2 sp, ch 3, sc in next ch-2 sp, ch 1, 7 dc in next ch-2 sp, ch 1, sc in next ch-2 sp, ch 3, *sh in next ch-2 sp, sc in next ch-3 sp, ch 3, sc in next ch-3 sp, sh in next ch-2 sp, ch 3, sc in next ch-2 sp, ch 1, 7 dc in next ch-2 sp, ch 1, sc in next ch-2 sp, ch 3; repeat from * around, join with sl st in top of beg-ch—32 sc, 56 dc (not including sts in shells), 16 sh.

Rnd 19: Sl st in each st to next ch-2 sp, beg-sh in same sp, ch 3, sc in next ch-3 sp, ch 3, sh in next ch-2 sp, ch 3, sk next 2 ch-sps, 2 dc in next dc, (dc in next st, 2 dc in next st) 3 times, *ch 3, sh in next ch-2 sp, ch 3, sc in next ch-3 sp, ch 3, sh in next ch-2 sp, ch 3, sk next 2 ch-sps, 2 dc in next dc, (dc in next st, 2 dc in next st) 3 times; repeat from * around, ch 3, join with sl st in top of beg-ch—88 dc (not including sts in shells), 16 sh.

Rnd 20: Sl st in each st to next ch-2 sp, (ch 3, dc, ch 2, 2 dc, ch 2, first-half-cl) in same sp, [second-half-cl, (ch 2, 2 dc) twice] in next ch-2 sp, ch 3, sk next ch-3 sp, dc in next dc, (ch 1, dc in next st) 10 times, ch 3, *[(2 dc, ch 2) twice, first-half-cl] in next ch-2 sp, [second-half-cl, (ch 2, 2 dc) twice] in next ch-2 sp, ch 3, sk next ch-3 sp, dc in next dc, (ch 1, dc in next st) 10 times, ch 3; repeat from * around, join with sl st in top of beg-ch—8 cl, 88 dc (not including sts in shells), 16 sh.

Rnd 21: Sl st in each st to next ch-2 sp, beg-sh in same sp, ch 1, first-half-cl in next ch-2 sp, second-half-cl in next ch-2 sp, ch 1, sh in next ch-2 sp, ch 3, sk next ch-3 sp, sc in next dc, (ch 3, sk next ch-1 sp, sc in next dc) 10 times, ch 3, *sh in next ch-2 sp, ch 1, first-half-cl in next ch-2 sp, second-half-cl in next ch-2 sp, ch 1, sh in next ch-2 sp, ch 3, sk next ch-3 sp, sc in next dc, (ch 3, sk next ch-1 sp, sc in next dc) 10 times, ch 3; repeat from * around, join with sl st in top of beg-ch—16 sh, 8 cl, 88 sc.

Rnd 22: Sl st in each st to next ch-2 sp, beg-sh in same sp, ch 5, sh in next ch-2 sp, ch 3, sk next ch-3 sp, (sc in next ch-3 sp, ch 3) 10 times, *sh in next ch-2 sp, ch 5, sh in next ch-2 sp, ch 3, sk next ch-3 sp, (sc in next ch-3 sp, ch 3) 10 times; repeat from * around, join with sl st in top of beg-ch—16 sh, 80 sc.

Rnd 23: Sl st in each st to next ch-2 sp, beg-sh in same sp, ch 2, sc in next ch-5 sp, ch 2, sh in next ch-2 sp, ch 3, sk next ch-3 sp, (sc in next ch-3 sp, ch 3) 9 times, *sh in next ch-2 sp, ch 2, sc in next ch-5 sp, ch 2, sh in next ch-2 sp, ch 3, sk next ch-3 sp, (sc in next ch-3 sp, ch 3) 9 times; repeat from * around, join with sl st in top of beg-ch—16 sh, 72 sc.

Rnd 24: Sl st in each st to next ch-2 sp, beg-sh in same sp, ch 3, 3 tr in next sc, ch 3, sk next ch-2 sp, sh in next ch-2 sp, ch 3, sk next ch-3 sp, (sc in next ch-3 sp, ch 3) 8 times, *sh in next ch-2 sp, ch 3, 3 tr in next sc, ch 3, sk next ch-2 sp, sh in next ch-2 sp, ch 3, sk next ch-3 sp, (sc in next ch-3 sp, ch 3) 8 times; repeat from * around, join with sl st in top of beg-ch—16 sh, 24 tr, 64 sc.

Rnd 25: Sl st in each st to next ch-2 sp, beg-sh in same sp, ch 1, [2 dc, (ch 2, 2 dc) 3 times] in center tr of next 3-tr group, ch 1, sh in next ch-2 sp, ch 3, sk next ch-3 sp, (sc in next ch-3 sp, ch 3) 7 times, *sh in next ch-2 sp, ch 1, [2 dc, (ch 2, 2 dc) 3 times) in center tr of next 3-tr group, ch 1, sh in next ch-2 sp, ch 3, sk next ch-3 sp, (sc in next ch-3 sp, ch 3) 7 times; repeat from * around, join with sl st in top of beg-ch—16 sh, 64 dc (not including sts in shells), 56 sc.

Rnd 26: Sl st in each st to next ch-2 sp, beg-sh in same sp, ch 1, sh in each of next 3 ch-2 sps, ch 1, sh in next ch-2 sp, ch 3, sk next ch-3 sp, (sc in next ch-3 sp, ch 3) 6 times, *sh in next ch-2 sp, ch 1, sh in each of next 3 ch-2 sps, ch 1, sh in next ch-2 sp, ch 3, sk next ch-3 sp, (sc in next ch-3 sp, ch 3) 6 times; repeat from * around, join with sl st in top of beg-ch—40 sh, 48 sc.

Rnd 27: Sl st in each st to next ch-2 sp, beg-sh in same sp, (ch 1, sh in next ch-2 sp) 4 times, ch 3, sk next ch-3 sp, (sc in next ch-3 sp, ch 3) 5 times, *sh in next ch-2 sp, (ch 1, sh in next ch-2 sp) 4 times, ch 3, sk next ch-3 sp, (sc in next ch-3 sp, ch 3) 5 times; repeat from * around, join with sl st in top of beg-ch—40 sh, 40 sc.

Rnd 28: Sl st in each st to next ch-2 sp, beg-sh in same sp, (ch 2, sh in next ch-2 sp) 4 times, ch 3, sk next ch-3 sp, (sc in next ch-3 sp, ch 3) 4 times, *sh in next ch-2 sp, (ch 2, sh in next ch-2 sp) 4 times, ch 3, sk next ch-3 sp, (sc in next ch-3 sp, ch 3) 4 times; repeat from * around, join with sl st in top of beg-ch—40 sh, 32 sc.

Rnd 29: Sl st in each st to next ch-2 sp, beg-sh in same sp, (ch 3, sk next ch-2 sp, sh in next ch-2 sp) 4 times, ch 3, sk next ch-3 sp, (sc in next ch-3 sp, ch 3) 3 times, *sh in next ch-2 sp, (ch 3, sk next ch-2 sp, sh in next ch-2 sp) 4 times, ch 3, sk next ch-3 sp, (sc in next

ch-3 sp, ch 3) 3 times; repeat from * around, join with sl st in top of beg-ch—40 sh, 24 sc.

Rnd 30: Sl st in each st to next ch-2 sp, beg-sh in same sp, ch 3, sh in next ch-2 sp, ch 1, [2 dc, (ch 2, 2 dc) 3 times] in next ch-2 sp, ch 1, sh in next ch-2 sp, ch 3, sh in next ch- 2 sp, ch 3, sk next ch-3 sp, (sc in next ch-3 sp, ch 3) twice, *sh in next ch-2 sp, ch 3, sh in next ch-2 sp, ch 1, [2 dc, (ch 2, 2 dc) 3 times] in next ch-2 sp, ch 1, sh in next ch-2 sp, ch 3, sh in next ch-2 sp, ch 3, sk next ch-3 sp, (sc in next ch-3 sp, ch 3) twice; repeat from * around, join with sl st in top of beg-ch—32 sh, 64 dc (not including sts in shells), 16 sc.

Rnd 31: Sl st in each st to next ch-2 sp, beg-sh in same sp, ch 3, sh in next ch-2 sp, ch 1, sh in each of next 3 ch-2 sps, ch 1, (sh in next ch-2 sp, ch 3) twice, sk next ch-3 sp, sc in next ch-3 sp, *(ch 3, sh in next ch-2 sp) twice, ch 1, sh in each of next 3 ch-2 sps, ch 1, (sh in next ch-2 sp, ch 3) twice, sk next ch-3 sp, sc in next ch-3 sp; repeat from * around, ch 3, join with sl st in top of beg-ch—56 sh, 8 sc.

Rnd 32: Sl st in each st to next ch-2 sp, beg-sh in same sp, ch 3, sh in next ch-2 sp, ch 2, (sh in next ch-2 sp, ch 1) twice, sh in next ch-2 sp, ch 2, sh in next ch-2 sp, ch 3, (sh, ch 2, first-half-cl) in next ch-2 sp, *(second-half-cl, ch 2, sh) in next ch-2 sp, ch 3, sh in next ch-2 sp, ch 2, (sh in next ch-2 sp, ch 1) twice, sh in next ch-2 sp, ch 2, sh in next ch-2 sp, ch 3, (sh, ch 2, first-half-cl) in next ch-2 sp; repeat from * around, second-half-cl in same ch-2 sp as beg-sh, ch 2, join with sl st in top of beg-ch—56 sh, 8 cl.

Rnd 33: Sl st in each st to next ch-2 sp, beg-sh in same sp, ch 3, sh in next ch-2 sp, ch 3, sk next ch-2 sp, sh in next ch-2 sp, (ch 3, sh in next ch-2 sp) twice, ch 3, sk next ch-2 sp, sh in next ch-2 sp, ch 3, sh in next ch-2 sp, ch 1, first-half-cl in next ch-2 sp, second-half-cl in next ch-2 sp, ch 1, *(sh in next ch-2 sp, ch 3) twice, ch 3, sk next ch-2 sp, sh in next ch-2 sp, (ch 3, sh in next ch-2 sp) twice, ch 3, sk next ch-2 sp, sh in next ch-2 sp, ch 3, sh in next ch-2 sp, ch 1, first-half-cl in next ch-2 sp, second-half-cl in next ch-2 sp, ch 1; repeat from * around, join with sl st in top of beg-ch—56 sh, 8 cl.

Rnd 34: Sl st in each st to next ch-2 sp, beg-sh in same sp, (ch 3, sh in next ch-2 sp) twice, ch 1, [2 dc, (ch 2,

2 dc) 3 times] in next ch-2 sp, *ch 1, (sh in next ch-2 sp, ch 3) 5 times, sh in next ch-2 sp, ch 1, [2 dc, (ch 2, 2 dc) 3 times] in next ch-2 sp: repeat from * around to last 3 ch-2 sps, ch 1, (sh in next ch-2 sp, ch 3) 3 times, join with sl st in top of beg-ch—48 sh, 64 dc.

Rnd 35: Sl st in each st to next ch-2 sp, beg-sh in same sp, (ch 3, sh in next ch-2 sp) twice, ch 1, sh in each of next 3 ch-2 sps, ch 1, (sh in next ch-2 sp, ch 3) twice, sh in next ch-2 sp, ch 1, sc in next ch-3 sp, ch 1, *(sh in next ch-2 sp, ch 3) twice, sh in next ch-2 sp, ch 1, sh in each of next 3 ch-2 sps, ch 1, (sh in next ch-2 sp, ch 3) twice, sh in next ch-2 sp, ch 1, sc in next ch-3 sp, ch 1; repeat from * around, join with sl st in top of beg-ch—72 sh, 8 sc.

Rnd 36: Sl st in each st to next ch-2 sp, beg-sh in same sp, (ch 3, sh in next ch-2 sp) 3 times, (ch 1, sh in next ch-2 sp) twice, ch 3, (sh in next ch-2 sp, ch 3) 3 times, 3 tr in next sc, ch 3, *(sh in next ch-2 sp, ch 3) 3 times, sh in next ch-2 sp, (ch 1, sh in next ch-2 sp) twice, ch 3, (sh in next ch-2 sp, ch 3) 3 times, 3 tr in next sc, ch 3; repeat from * around, join with sl st in top of beg-ch—81 sh, 24 tr.

Rnd 37: Sl st in each st to next ch-2 sp, beg-sh in same sp, (ch 3, sh in next ch-2 sp) 8 times, ch 1, [2 dc, (ch 2, 2 dc) 3 times] in center tr of next 3-tr group, ch 1, *(sh in next ch-2 sp, ch 3) 8 times, sh in next ch-2 sp, ch 1, [2 dc, (ch 2, 2 dc) 3 times] in center tr of next 3-tr group, ch 1; repeat from * around, join with sl st in top of beg-ch—81 sh, 64 dc (not including sts in shells).

Rnd 38: Sl st in each st to next ch-2 sp, beg-sh in same sp, (ch 3, sh in next ch-2 sp) 8 times, ch 1, sh in each of next 3 ch-2 sps, ch 1, *sh in next ch-2 sp, (ch 3, sh in next ch-2 sp) 8 times, ch 1, sh in each of next 3 ch-2 sps, ch 1; repeat from * around, join with sl st in top of beg-ch—96 sh.

Rnd 39: Sl st in each st to next ch-2 sp, beg-sh in same sp, ch 3, (sh in next ch-2 sp, ch 3) 8 times, sh in next ch-2 sp, (ch 1, sh in next ch-2 sp) twice, ch 3, *(sh in next ch-2 sp, ch 3) 9 times, sh in next ch-2 sp, (ch 1, sh in next ch-2 sp) twice, ch 3; repeat from * around, join with sl st in top of beg-ch—96 sh.

Rnd 40: Sl st in each st to next ch-2 sp, beg-sh in same sp, ch 3, (sh in next ch-2 sp, ch 3) around, join with sl st in top of beg-ch.

Rnd 41: Sl st in each st to next ch-2 sp, ch 3 (counts as dc), 2 dc in same sp, 3 dc in each ch-3 and ch-2 sp around, join with sl st in top of beg-ch.

Rnd 42: Ch 3, 2 dc in next st, *dc in next st, 2 dc in next st; repeat from * around, join with sl st in top of beg-ch, fasten off.

Finishing

With a yarn needle, weave in ends. Immerse the piece in cool water, then squeeze out the excess water, taking care not to wring or twist. Place the piece on a towel on a flat surface and gently stretch to open up the lace pattern. Leave until completely dry.

Motifs

A motif is a distinctive and recurring form, shape, or figure in a design. One of the most popular motifs in crochet is the granny square, but motifs can also be octagons, pentagons, triangles, and circles. To make a project built from motifs, you crochet each motif individually, then join them, either all at once at the end or as you make them. I'm not a big fan of sewing, so two of the motif designs are assembled using a "join-as-you-go" technique that works up quite quickly. It may sound complicated in writing, so I have included a tutorial with step-by-step photos (see page 82).

Lacy motifs are some of my favorite things to design. I hope you enjoy them too!

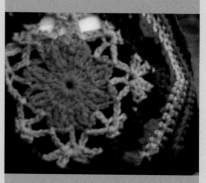

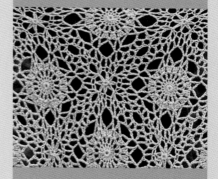

Midnight Azaleas

SKILL LEVEL

EASY

Don't let the complexity of this wrap intimidate you! Take it one step at a time and you will surprise yourself with your abilities. Simple blocks are made in an assortment of colors and sewn together. A basic border is worked across the top, with a traditional ripple worked along the bottom edge.

FINISHED SIZE

65 in./165 cm wide by 21 in./53.5 cm long

YARN

Cascade Yarns Greenland (100% Merino Superwash; 3.5 oz/100 g, 137 yd./125 m ball):

1 ball #3556 Amethyst (A)

1 ball #3516 Magenta (B)

2 balls #3526 Granny Smith (C)

2 balls #3542 Olive Heather (D)

3 balls #3503 Black (E)

CROCHET HOOK

US J-10 (6 mm) or size needed to obtain gauge

ADDITIONAL MATERIALS

Yarn needle

GAUGE

Rnds 1 and 2 = 4 in./10 cm; 12 sts and 13 rows = 4 in./10 cm

Special Stitches

Cl (Cluster): *Yarn over 2 times, insert hook in indicated stitch, pull up loop (4 loops on hook), [yarn over, pull through 2 loops on hook] 2 times (2 loops remain on hook); repeat from * with 5 loops on hook after first step and 3 loops on hook after second step, yarn over and pull through all 3 loops on hook.

Dc2tog (Double crochet 2 together): [Yarn over, insert hook in next stitch and draw up a loop, yarn over and draw through 2 loops on hook] twice, yarn over and draw through all 3 loops on hook.

Sc2tog (Single crochet 2 together): [Insert hook in next stitch, yarn over and draw up a loop] twice, yarn over and draw through all 3 loops on hook.

Sh (Shell): Work 5 tr in indicated space or stitch.

V-st (V-stitch): (Dc, ch 3, dc) in same stitch.

> **NOTE** Do not turn at end of rounds; work with RS facing at all times unless instructed otherwise.

Instructions

Block A *(make 4)*

With A, ch 5, join with sl st to form ring.

Rnd 1 (RS): Ch 3 (counts as first dc here and throughout), 15 dc in ring, join with sl st in top of beg ch—16 dc.

Rnd 2: Ch 1, sc in first same st as join, ch 3, Cl in next st, ch 3, *sc in next st, ch 3, Cl in next st, ch 3; repeat from * 7 times, join with sl st in beg sc, fasten off—8 sc, 8 Cl.

Rnd 3: Join C with sl st in any sc, ch 7 (counts as tr, ch 3), sl st in top of next Cl, ch 3, *tr in next sc, ch 3, sl st in top of next Cl, ch 3; repeat from * around, join with sl st in 4th ch of beg ch-7—8 sl st, 8 tr.

Rnd 4: Ch 3, (2 dc, ch 3, 3 dc) in same st as join (corner made), ch 3, 5 sc in next tr, ch 3, *(3 dc, ch 3, 3 dc) in next tr (corner made), ch 3, 5 sc in next tr, ch 3; repeat from * around, join with sl st in top of beg ch, fasten off—24 dc, 20 sc.

Rnd 5: Join D with sl st in any corner ch-3 sp, ch 3, 4 dc in same sp, sk next st, sc in next st (center dc of a 3-dc group), 3 dc in next ch-3 sp, sk next 2 sts, sc in next st (center sc of a 5-sc group), 3 dc in next ch-3 sp, sk next st, sc in next st, *5 dc in next ch-3 sp, sk next st, sc in next st, 3 dc in next ch-3 sp, sk next 2 sts, sc in next st, 3 dc in next ch-3 sp, sk next st, sc in next st; repeat from * around, join with sl st in top of beg ch, fasten off—44 dc, 12 sc.

Rnd 6: Join E with sl st in first dc of any 5-dc corner, ch 1, sc in same st, sc in next 4 dc, V-st in next sc, [sc in next 3 dc, V-st in next sc] 2 times, *sc in next 5 dc, V-st in next sc, [sc in next 3 dc, V-st in next sc] 2 times; repeat from * around, join with sl st in beg sc, fasten off leaving a long length for sewing—44 sc, 12 V-sts.

Block B (make 3)

Rnds 1 and 2: With B, repeat Rnds 1 and 2 of Block A.
Rnds 3 and 4: With D, repeat Rnds 3 and 4 of Block A.
Rnd 5: With C, repeat Rnd 5 of Block A.
Rnd 6: With E, repeat Rnd 6 for Block A.

Assembly

With yarn needle, using long yarn length at end of Rnd 6, sew a corner of a Block A to a corner of a Block B, beginning at center ch of the ch-3 sp before the corner, including 7 sts, and then up to center ch of next ch-3 sp following corner. Continue in same manner alternating colors until all blocks are joined into a long strip.

Top Border

Row 1: With RS facing, join E with sl st in ch-3 sp of first V-st at beginning of top edge (you are beginning in the first "valley"), ch 3 (counts as dc), sk next 2 sts, 3 dc in next st, sc in next ch-3 sp, sk next 2 sts, *3 dc in next st, (sc, ch 3, sc) in next ch-3 sp, sk next st, sc in next 5 sts, (sc, ch 3, sc) in next ch-3 sp, sk next 2 sts, 3 dc in next st, 3 dc in next ch-3 sp, sk next 2 sts, dc in next st, sh in center of block joining, sk next 2 sts, dc in next st, 3 dc in next ch-3 sp, sk next 2 sts; repeat from * 5 more times, 3 dc in next st, (sc, ch 3, sc) in next ch-3 sp, sk next st, sc in next 5 sts, (sc, ch 3, sc) in next ch-3 sp, sk next 2 sts, 3 dc in next st, sc in next ch-3 sp, sk next 2 sts, 3 dc in next st, dc in next ch-3 sp, turn.

Row 2: Ch 1, sc in first 8 sts,*(sc, ch 3, sc) in next ch-3 sp, sk next st, sc in next 5 sts, (sc, ch 3, sc) in next ch-3 sp, sk next st, dc in next 5 sts, sh in center st of next sh, sk next 4 sts, dc in next 5 sts; repeat from * 5 more times, (sc, ch 3, sc) in next ch-3 sp, sk next st, sc in next 5 sts, (sc, ch 3, sc) in next ch-3 sp, sk next st, sc in last 8 sts, turn.

Row 3: Ch 1, [sc in each st up to next ch-3 sp, (sc, ch 3, sc) in next ch-3 sp] twice, *sk next st, dc in next 3 sts, sh in center st of next sh, sk next 4 sts, dc in next 3 sts, (sc , ch 3, sc) in next ch-3 sp, sc in each st up to next ch-3 sp, (sc, ch 3, sc) in next ch-3 sp; repeat from * 5 more times, sc in each st to end, turn.

Row 4: Ch 1, [sc in each st up to next ch-3 sp, 3 sc in next ch-3 sp] twice, *sk next st, tr in next 2 sts, sh in center st of next sh, sk next 3 sts, tr in next 2 sts, 3 sc in next ch-3 sp, sc in each st up to next ch-3 sp, 3 sc in next ch-3 sp; repeat from * 5 more times, sc in each st to end, turn.

Row 5: Ch 1, sc in each st to end, fasten off.

Bottom Ripple

Row 1: With RS facing, working across opposite side of strip, join B with sc in ch-3 sp of first V-st at beginning of bottom edge, *[sk next 2 sts, 3 dc in next sc, sc in next ch-3 sp] 2 times, sk next st, sc in next 2 sc, 5 sc in next sc, sc in next 2 sc, [sc in next ch-3 sp, sk next 2 sts, 3 dc in next sc] 2 times, 3 dc in center of motif joining; repeat from * 5 more times, [sk next 2 sts, 3 dc in next sc, sc in next ch-3 sp] 2 times, sk next st, sc in next 2 sc, 5 sc in next sc, sc in next 2 sc, [sc in next ch-3 sp, sk next 2 sts, 3 dc in next sc] 2 times, sc in next ch-3 sp, fasten off—93 sc, 102 dc.

Row 2: With RS facing, join C with sc in first st, sc2tog, sc in next 10 sts, *3 sc in next st, sc in next 11 sts, sc2tog, sc in next st, sc2tog, sc in next 11 sts; repeat from * 5 more times, 3 sc in next st, sc in next 10 sts, sc2tog, sc in last st, fasten off—195 sc.

Row 3: With A, repeat Row 2.

Row 4: With D, repeat Row 2.

Row 5: With B, repeat Row 2.

Row 6: With RS facing, join E with sl st in first st, ch 3, dc2tog, dc in next 10 sts, *3 dc in next st, dc in next 11 sts, dc2tog, dc in next st, dc2tog, dc in next 11 sts; repeat from * 5 more times, 3 dc in next st, dc in next 10 sts, dc2tog, dc in last st, turn.

Row 7: Ch 1, sc in first st, sc2tog, sc in next 10 sts, *3 sc in next st, sc in next 11 sts, sc2tog, sc in next st, sc2tog, sc in next 11 sts; repeat from * 5 more times, 3 sc in next st, sc in next 10 sts, sc2tog, sc in last st, turn.

Row 8: Ch 3, dc2tog, dc in next 10 sts, *3 dc in next st, dc in next 11 sts, dc2tog, dc in next st, dc2tog, dc in next 11 sts; repeat from * 5 more times, 3 dc in next st, dc in next 10 sts, dc2tog, dc in last st, fasten off.

Row 9: With B, repeat Row 2.

Rows 10–17: Repeat Rows 2–9.

Rows 18–21: Repeat Rows 2–5.

Edging

Row 1: Join E with sc in first row; work evenly spaced sc across short side. Repeat for opposite side.

Finishing

With a yarn needle, weave in ends. Immerse the piece in cool water, then squeeze out the excess water, taking care not to wring or twist. Place the piece on a towel on a flat surface and gently stretch to open up the lace pattern around the flower. Leave until completely dry.

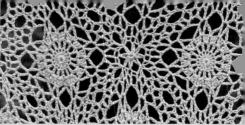

Waiting for Willow

As I stitched this shawl, my thoughts wandered to another fascinating creation, my granddaughter Willow, who would be born a few months later. Using a "join-as-you-go" technique allowed me to create this stunning shawl with a touch of mystery. I love the look of the lace and the ease of assembly. I hope you do, too!

FINISHED SIZE

Each front panel = 17 in./43 cm across, front to back = 39 in./99 cm

YARN

Aunt Lydia's Iced Bamboo; (96% Viscose from Bamboo, 4% Metallic; 1.86 oz/53 g, 100 yd./91 m ball):

6 balls #3501 Aqua Ice

CROCHET HOOK

US F/5 (3.75 mm) or size needed to obtain gauge

ADDITIONAL MATERIALS

Yarn needle

GAUGE

Unjoined motif = 6 in./15 cm; joined motifs = 6½ in./16.5 cm

Special Stitches

Ch-3 join (Chain 3 join): Ch 1, drop loop from hook, insert hook in corresponding ch-3 space, pick up dropped loop and pull through, ch 1.

Sh (Shell): 3 dc in indicated stitch.

V-st (V-stitch): (Dc, ch 3, dc) in indicated space.

> **NOTE** Motifs are worked and joined as you go in the order indicated in the assembly diagram.

Instructions

Strip 1 (Motifs 1–6)

MOTIF 1

Ch 4, join with sl st to form ring.

Rnd 1: Ch 3 (counts as dc here and throughout), 15 dc in ring, join with sl st st in top of beg-ch—16 dc.

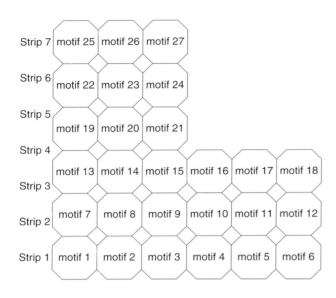

Rnd 2: Ch 4 (counts as dc, ch 1 here and throughout), *dc in next st, ch 1; repeat from * around, join with sl st st in 3rd ch of beg ch-4—16 dc, 16 ch-1 sps.

Rnd 3: (Sl st, ch 3, 2 dc) in next ch-1 sp (first shell made), sh in each ch-1 sp around, join with sl st in top of beg ch-3—16 sh.

Rnd 4: Ch 6 (counts as dc, ch 3 here and throughout), dc in same st as joining (first V-st made), ch 3, sk next sh, sl st in sp before next sh, ch 3, sk next sh, *V-st in sp before next sh, ch 3, sk next sh, sl st in sp before next sh, ch 3; repeat from * around, join with sl st in 3rd ch of beg ch-6—8 V-sts, 8 sl sts.

Rnd 5: [Sl st, ch 6, dc, (ch 3, dc) twice] in ch-3 sp of first V-st, ch 1, *[dc, (ch 3, dc) 3 times] in ch-3 sp of next V-st, ch 1; repeat from * around, join with sl st in 3rd ch of beg ch-6—32 dc, 24 ch-3 sp.

Rnd 6: Sl st in next ch-3 sp, ch 6, dc in same sp, (hdc, ch 3, hdc) in next ch-3 sp, V-st in next ch-3 sp, tr in next ch-1 sp, *V-st in next ch-3 sp, (hdc, ch 3, hdc) in next ch-3 sp, V-st in next ch-3 sp, tr in next ch-1 sp; repeat from * around, join with sl st in 3rd ch of beg ch-6—24 ch-3 sps. Fasten off.

MOTIF 2

Work same as motif 1 through Rnd 5—32 dc, 24 ch-3 sp. Hold motif 1 and motif 2 with WS together and stitches matching.

Rnd 6 (join to one previous motif): Sl st in next ch-3 sp, ch 6, dc in same sp, (hdc, ch 3, hdc) in next ch-3 sp, V-st in next ch-3 sp, tr in next ch-1 sp; join motif 2 to motif 1 across one edge as follows: [(dc, ch-3 join, dc) in next ch-3 sp, (hdc, ch-3 join, hdc) in next ch-3 sp, (dc, ch-3 join, dc) in next ch-3 sp, tr in next ch-1 sp] twice; complete motif 2 as follows: *V-st in next ch-3 sp, (hdc, ch 3, hdc) in next ch-3 sp, V-st in next ch-3 sp, tr in next ch-1 sp; repeat from * around, join with sl st in 3rd ch of beg ch-6. Fasten off.

MOTIFS 3–6

Work same as motif 2, joining each motif to previous motif to form a long strip.

Strip 2 (Motifs 7–12)

MOTIF 7

Work same as motif 2, joining motif 7 to motif 1 to begin next row of motifs.

MOTIF 8

Work same as motif 1 through Rnd 5—32 dc, 24 ch-3 sp.

Hold motif 8 and motif 7 with WS together and stitches matching.

Rnd 6 (join to two previous motifs): Sl st in next ch-3 sp, ch 6, dc in same sp, (hdc, ch 3, hdc) in next ch-3 sp, V-st in next ch-3 sp, tr in next ch-1 sp; join motif 8 to motif 7 across one edge as follows: *[(dc, ch-3 join, dc) in next ch-3 sp, (hdc, ch-3 join, hdc) in next ch-3 sp, (dc, ch-3 join, dc) in next ch-3 sp, tr in next ch-1 sp] twice; hold motif 8 and motif 2 with WS together and sts matching, repeat from * to join motifs across one edge; complete motif 8 as follows: *V-st in next ch-3 sp, (hdc, ch 3, hdc) in next ch-3 sp, V-st in next ch-3 sp, tr in next ch-1 sp; repeat from * around, join with sl st in 3rd ch of beg ch-6.

MOTIFS 9–12

Work same as motif 8, joining each motif to previous motif and next motif of Strip 1.

Strip 3 (Motifs 13–18)

Work and join same as Strip 2, joining to Strip 2.

Strip 4 (Motifs 19–21)

Work same as motifs 7–9 of Strip 2, joining to first 3 motifs of Strip 3.

Strip 5 (Motifs 22–24)

Work same as Strip 4, joining to Strip 4.

Strip 6 (Motifs 25–27)

Work same as Strip 5, joining to Strip 5.

Filler Motifs

Ch 4, join with sl st to form ring.

Hold filler motif in an opening between joined large motifs.

Rnd 1: [Ch 2, sl st in edge of opening, ch 2, sl st in ring] 8 times, spacing the joins evenly around edge of opening. Fasten off.

Fill each gap between large motifs with a filler motif (16 filler motifs in all).

Finishing

With a yarn needle, weave in ends. Immerse the piece in cool water, then squeeze out the excess water, taking care not to wring or twist. Place the piece on a towel on a flat surface and gently stretch to open up the lace pattern. Leave until completely dry.

Mystic Stars

SKILL LEVEL

■■■■▬

EXPERIENCED

Wrap yourself in this beautiful shawl as you take a moon-light stroll along the beach under twinkling stars that have been recreated in the star-shaped motifs of this project. Although the shawl uses both large motifs and filler motifs, it is not as complicated as it may appear. Crochet and assemble the large motifs first, then go back and work the filler motifs directly into the openings created as you assembled the large motifs. You will find this makes it very clear to see where to work the joining stitches.

FINISHED SIZE

21¾ in./55 cm across each front by 43½ in./110 cm long

YARN

Drops Delight from Garnstudio; (75% Wool Superwash, 25% Polyamide); 1.76 oz/50 g, 191 yd./175 m ball):

5 balls #11 Lilac/Green

CROCHET HOOK

US F-5 (3.75 mm) or size needed to obtain gauge

ADDITIONAL MATERIALS

Yarn needle

GAUGE

Star Motif = 7¼ in./18.5 cm

Special Stitches

Beg ch-5 join (Beginning ch-5 join): Ch 5, drop loop from hook, insert hook in center chain of any ch-5 space in opening between Star Motifs, pick up dropped loop and pull through, ch 2.

Ch-3 join (Chain 3 join): Ch 1, drop loop from hook, insert hook in next ch-3 space of opening between Star Motifs, pick up dropped loop and pull through, ch 1.

Ch-5 join (Chain 5 join): Ch 2, drop loop from hook, insert hook in center chain of next ch-5 space of opening between Star Motifs, pick up dropped loop and pull through, ch 2.

NOTES

1. Do not turn at end of rounds.
2. In Round 4 you will be instructed to ch 7 and then work sts into the chain which was just made to create the points of the star.
3. In Round 5 you will be instructed to work in the bottom loops of the ch from Round 4, you will then ch 3 and begin working in the top of the stitches from Round 4 that were worked into the chs, outlining the points of the star.

Instructions

Strip 1 (stars 1–6)

STAR 1

Ch 5, join with sl st to form ring.

Rnd 1 (RS): Ch 1, 16 sc in ring, join with sl st in beg-sc—
16 sc.

Rnd 2: Ch 6 (counts as dc, ch 3), sk next st, *dc in next
st, ch 3, sk next st; repeat from * around, join with sl
st in 3rd ch of beg ch-6—8 dc, 8 ch-3 sps.

Rnd 3: Sl st in next ch-3 sp, ch 3 (counts as dc), 4 dc in
same ch-3 sp, ch 1, *5 dc in next ch-3 sp, ch 1; repeat
from * around, join with sl st in top of beg-ch—40 dc,
8 ch-1 sps.

Rnd 4: Ch 1, sc in last ch-1 sp (just before the joining),
ch 7, sc in 2nd ch from hook, hdc in next ch, dc in
next ch, tr in next 3 ch (point made), *sc in next ch-1
sp, ch 7, sc in 2nd ch from hook, hdc in next ch, dc in
next ch, tr in next 3 ch (point made); repeat from *
around, join with sl st in beg-sc—16 sc, 8 hdc, 8 dc,
24 tr (8 points).

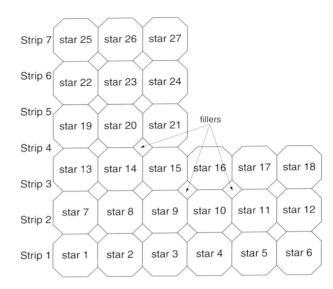

Rnd 5: Ch 1, sc in same st as joining, working in bottom
loops of ch of Rnd 4, sc in each ch to "tip" of point
(do not sc in the skipped ch at the "tip"), ch 3, *sc in
next 6 sts down other side of point, sc in sc between
points, sc in next 6 ch to "tip" of next point, ch 3;
repeat from * 6 more times, sc in next 6 sts down side
of last point, join with sl st in beg-sc—104 sc, 8 ch-3
sp.

Rnd 6: Ch 9 (counts as tr, ch 5), tr in same st as joining,
ch 3, [sc, (ch 3, sc) 3 times] in next ch-3 sp, ch 3, *sk
next 6 sts, (tr, ch 5, tr) in next st, ch 3, [sc (ch 3, sc) 3
times] in next ch-3 sp, ch 3; repeat from * around,
join with sl st in 4th ch of beg ch-9—32 sc, 16 tr.

STAR 2

Work same as Star 1 through Rnd 5—32 sc, 16 tr.

Hold Star 1 and Star 2 with WS together and stitches
matching.

Rnd 6 (join to one previous star): Ch 9 (counts as tr, ch
5), tr in same st as joining, ch 3; join star 2 to star 1 as
follows: [sc, ch 3, sc, (ch-3 join, sc) twice] in next ch-3
sp, ch 3, sk next 6 sts, (tr, ch-5 join, tr) in next st, ch 3,
[(sc, ch-3 join) twice, sc, ch 3, sc] in next ch-3 sp, ch 3;
complete star 2 as follows: *sk next 6 sts, (tr, ch 5, tr)
in next st, ch 3, [sc, (ch 3, sc) 3 times] in next ch-3 sp,
ch 3; repeat from * around, join with sl st in 4th ch of
beg ch-9.

STARS 3–6

Work same as Star 2, joining each star to previous star to form a long strip.

Strip 2 (Stars 7–12)

STAR 7

Work same as Star 2, joining Star 7 to Star 1 to begin next row of stars.

STAR 8

Work same as Star 1 through Rnd 5—32 sc, 16 tr.

Hold Star 8 and Star 7 with WS together and stitches matching.

Rnd 6 (join to two previous stars): Ch 9 (counts as tr, ch 5), tr in same st, ch 3; join star 8 to star 7 as follows: [sc, ch 3, sc, (ch-3 join, sc) twice] in next ch-3 sp, ch 3, sk next 6 sts, (tr, ch-5 join, tr) in next st, ch 3, [(sc, ch-3 join) twice, sc, ch 3, sc] in next ch-3 sp; continue with star 8: ch 3, sk next 6 sts, (tr, ch 5, tr) in next st, ch 3; hold star 8 and star 2 with WS together and sts matching, join stars as follows: [sc, ch 3, sc, (ch-3 join, sc) twice] in next ch-3 sp, ch 3, sk next 6 sts, (tr, ch-5 join, tr) in next st, ch 3, [(sc, ch-3 join) twice, sc, ch 3, sc] in next ch-3 sp, ch 3; complete star 8 as follows: *sk next 6 sts, (tr, ch 5, tr) in next st, ch 3, [sc, (ch 3, sc) 3 times] in next ch-3 sp, ch 3; repeat from * around, join with sl st in 4th ch of beg ch-9.

STARS 9–12

Work same as Star 8, joining each star to previous star and next star of Strip 1.

Strip 3 (Stars 13–18)

Work and join same as Strip 2, joining to Strip 2.

Strip 4 (Stars 19–21)

Work same as Stars 7–9 of Strip 2, joining to first 3 motifs of Strip 3.

Strip 5 (Stars 22–24)

Work same as Strip 4, joining to Strip 4.

Strip 6 (Stars 25–27)

Work same as Strip 5, joining to Strip 5.

Filler Motif (make 16)

Ch 5, join with sl st to form ring.

Rnd 1: Ch 5 (counts as dc, ch 2), (dc in ring, ch 2) 11 times, join with sl st in 3rd ch of beg ch-5 – 12 dc, 12 ch-2 sps.

NOTE In Rnd 2, filler motif is joined to unworked ch-5 and ch-3 sps around outer edge of opening between star motifs. Only work into ch-sps of opening when instructed to do so (e.g. working ch-3 or ch-5 joins), otherwise work into the ch-sps of Rnd 1.

Rnd 2: (Sl st, beg ch-5, tr) in next ch-2 sp, (dc, ch-3 join, dc) in next ch-2 sp, sk next ch-3 sp of opening between star motifs, (dc, ch-3 join, dc) in next ch-2 sp , *(tr, ch-5 join, tr) in next ch-2 sp, (dc, ch-3 join, dc) in next ch-2 sp, sk next ch-3 sp of opening between star motifs, (dc, ch-3 join, dc) in next ch-2 sp; repeat from * around, join with sl st in 4th ch of beg ch-6. Fasten off.

Border

Rnd 1: With RS facing, join yarn with sl st in any st on outer edge of shawl, ch 3 (counts as dc), dc in each st and ch-sp around, join with sl st in top of beg-ch, fasten off.

Finishing

With a yarn needle, weave in ends. Immerse the piece in cool water, then squeeze out the excess water, taking care not to wring or twist. Place the piece on a towel on a flat surface and gently stretch to open up the lace pattern. Leave until completely dry.

Hairpin Lace

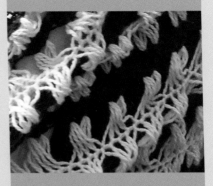

Also known as hairpin crochet, Maltese lace, Maltese work, fork work, fourche work, krotchee crochet, and Portuguese lace, this technique is believed to have been created in Victorian times. It was originally done on large U-shaped hairpins; this is where it gets its most common name. Today hairpin lace is worked on a loom that consists of two parallel rods that are held together at the top and bottom by removable bars. The lace is created by wrapping yarn around the rods to form loops, then crocheting in the centers of the loops with various stitches. This vertical row of stitches in the center is called the "spine." The strips of lace are removed from the loom once they reach the desired length and are assembled in many different ways. The technique yields a lightweight, airy fabric. See page 84 for step-by-step instructions with photos.

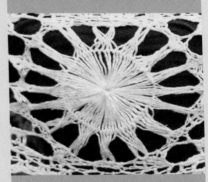

Shimmering Pearls

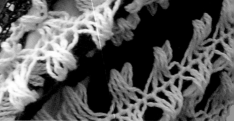

If you're looking for an elegant shawl to make in a hurry, then this is the pattern for you! Open and airy hairpin lace panels work up quickly and are then sewn together. Experiment with size and make as many or as few as you like to achieve the look that is right for you. Just one panel would make a stunning scarf.

FINISHED SIZE

26½ in./67.5 cm wide by 83 in./211 cm long

YARN

Lion Brand LB Collection Angora Merino; (80% Extrafine Merino Wool, 20% Angora; 1.75 oz/50 g, 131 yd./120 m ball):

4 balls #150 Smoked Pearl (MC)

4 balls #153 Black Velvet (CC)

CROCHET HOOK

US J-10 (6 mm) or size needed to obtain gauge

ADDITIONAL MATERIALS

Hairpin lace loom

Yarn needle

GAUGE

18 loops (9 on each side) = 4 in./10 cm

Instructions

Set the hairpin lace loom at 4¾ in. (12 cm). Make 5 strips of hairpin lace 176 loops long.

Strip Edging

Row 1: With CC, insert hook in first 4 loops held together as one, ch 3 (counts as dc), 3 dc in same set of loops, *4 dc in next set of 4 loops; repeat from * across, fasten off leaving a long length for sewing. Repeat across second side of strip.

Assembly

Matching up stitches of strip edging, whipstitch strips together loosely with a yarn needle.

Final Edging

Row 1: With RS facing, join CC with slip st in first st on either outside edge, ch 3 (counts as dc), dc in each st across, fasten off. Repeat for opposite outside edge.

Finishing

With a yarn needle, weave in ends. Immerse the piece in cool water, then squeeze out the excess water, taking care not to wring or twist. Place the piece on a towel on a flat surface and gently stretch to open up the lace pattern. Leave until completely dry.

Irish Jig

What a versatile piece this is! Not only can it be worn as a shawl but it also looks fantastic worn over your favorite skirt or dress. It's hard to have it on and not want to spin around and dance. It's a very fun piece with lots of movement.

FINISHED SIZE

18 in./45.5 cm wide; 40 in./101.5 cm top diameter; 78 in./198 cm bottom diameter

YARN

Interlacements Irish Jig; (40% Flax, 31% Cotton, 29% Rayon with Metallic Thread; 8 oz/227 g, 600 yd./549 m hank):

2 hanks Carbon Dioxide

CROCHET HOOK

US G-6 (4 mm) or size needed to obtain gauge

ADDITIONAL MATERIALS

Hairpin lace loom

Yarn needle

GAUGE

17 sc and 16 sc rows = 4 in./10 cm

> **NOTES**
> 1. Six solid panels and five hairpin lace panels are joined alternately to form the shawl.
> 2. The shawl can be made larger if desired by adding one additional hairpin lace panel and one additional solid panel.

Instructions

Set the hairpin lace loom at 4¾ in. (12 cm). Make 5 strips of hairpin lace 78 loops long.

Solid Panel (make 6)

Row 1: Ch 6, sc in 2nd ch from hook and each ch across—5 sc.

Rows 2–6: Ch 1, turn, sc in each st across.

Row 7: Ch 1, turn, 2 sc in first st, sc in each st up to last st, 2 sc in last st—7 sc.

Rows 8–12: Repeat Rows 2–6.

Rows 13–78: Repeat Rows 7–12 eleven times ending with 29 sc.

Edging rnd: Ch 1, pivot to work down long side edge, sc in end of each row, ch 1, pivot to work in bottom loops of Row 1, sc in each loop, ch 1, pivot to work up opposite long side edge, sc in end of each row, ch 1, sc in each st across last row of panel, ch 1, join with sl st in beg sc, fasten off—190 sc, 4 ch-1 sps.

Assembly

Place one solid panel and one hairpin lace panel side by side.

Joining Row: Join yarn with sc in ch-1 sp at lower corner of solid panel, sc in next st, ch 2, drop loop from hook, insert hook in next 3 loops on hairpin lace panel, pick up dropped loop, pull through, ch 2, *sk next st of solid panel, sc in next 2 sts, ch 2, drop loop from hook, insert hook in next 3 loops on hairpin lace panel, pick up dropped loop, pull through, ch 2; repeat from * 24 more times, sk next st of solid panel, sc in last st, sc in ch-1 sp, fasten off—54 sc.

Place another hairpin lace panel on the other side of the solid panel. Join yarn with a sc in ch-1 sp at the top corner of the solid panel and repeat Joining Row.

Continue to attach panels, alternating solid panels and hairpin lace panels until all 11 panels have been joined.

Finishing

With a yarn needle, weave in ends. Immerse the piece in cool water, then squeeze out the excess water, taking care not to wring or twist. Place the piece on a towel on a flat surface and gently stretch to open up the lace pattern. Leave until completely dry.

You Are My Sunshine

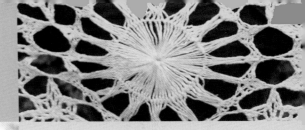

I know everyone has had that wonderful experience when the yarn speaks to you, dictating what it would like to be. Need I say more? Hairpin lace worked in the round creates perfect little sunshines for this whimsical shawl. It would be equally gorgeous worked in any color you like.

FINISHED SIZE

15 in./38 cm wide by 68½ in./174 cm long

YARN

Marigold Duke Silk; (100% Mulberry Silk; 3.50 oz/
100 g, 250 yd./220 m hank):

3 hanks Yellow

SKILL LEVEL

Experienced

CROCHET HOOK

US I-9 (5.5 mm) or size needed to obtain gauge

ADDITIONAL MATERIALS

Hairpin lace loom

Yarn needle

GAUGE

15 dc = 4 in./10 cm, hairpin motif = 9¾ in./
25 cm across

Special Stitches

Motif-join: Drop loop from hook, insert hook in center
chain of corresponding ch-space, pick up dropped
loop and pull through.

V-st (V-stitch): (Dc, ch 2, dc) in same stitch or space.

NOTES

1. Shawl is made from five large motifs that are
   joined as you go into a long strip. Filler motifs
   are worked and joined into the spaces between
   large motifs across each side edge.
2. Do not turn at end of rounds.

Instructions

Set the hairpin lace loom at 4¾ in. (12 cm). Make 5
strips of hairpin lace 80 loops long.

Grasp both ends of the guide yarn on one side of a
strip and pull tightly, gathering the loops together to
form the center of a circle. Knot the guide yarn to hold
in place. Fasten off, leaving a long length. Repeat with
the other 4 strips.

Motif 1

Rnd 1: Working over free loops around outside of circle,
holding 5 loops together as one, join yarn with sl st
in any set of loops, ch 3 (counts as first dc here and
throughout), 4 dc in same set of loops, *5 dc in next
set of 5 loops; repeat from * around, join with sl st in
top of beg-ch—80 dc.

Rnd 2: Ch 3, dc in next st, (2 dc, ch 3, 2 dc) in next st, dc in next 2 sts, sc in next 2 sts, ch 5, sk next st, sc in next 2 sts, *dc in next 2 sts, (2 dc, ch 3, 2 dc) in next st, dc in next 2 sts, sc in next 2 sts, ch 5, sk next st, sc in next 2 sts; repeat from * around, join with sl st in top of beg-ch, fasten off—64 dc, 32 sc.

Motif 2

Rnd 1: Work same as Rnd 1 of Motif 1.

Hold Motif 1 and Motif 2 with WS together and stitches matching.

Rnd 2: Ch 3, dc in next st, (2 dc, ch 1, motif-join, ch 1, 2 dc) in next st, dc in next 2 sts, sc in next 2 sts, ch 2, Motif-join, ch 2, sk next st, sc in next 2 sts, dc in next 2 sts, (2 dc, ch 1, motif-join, ch 1, 2 dc) in next st, dc in next 2 sts, sc in next 2 sts, ch 5, sk next st, sc in next 2 sts, *dc in next 2 sts, (2 dc, ch 3, 2 dc) in next st, dc in next 2 sts, sc in next 2 sts, ch 5, sk next st, sc in next 2 sts; repeat from * around, join with sl st in top of beg-ch, fasten off—64 dc, 32 sc.

Motifs 3–5

Work same as Motif 2, joining each motif to previous motif to form a long strip.

Filler Motif

Row 1: Ch 2, 9 sc in 2nd ch from hook, turn—9 sc.

Row 2: Ch 5 (counts as dc, ch 2), dc in first sc (first V-st made), *sk next st, V-st in next st; repeat from * to end, turn—5 V-sts.

Hold filler motif in one opening between joined large motifs across a long side of shawl.

Row 3: Sl st in ch-sp of first V-st, ch 3 (counts as hdc, ch 1), (motif-join, ch 1, hdc) in same sp, ch 3, sl st in sp before next V-st, ch 3, (hdc, ch 1, motif-join, ch 1, hdc) in ch-sp of next V-st, ch 3, sl st in sp before next V-st, ch 3, (dc, motif-join, dc) in ch-sp of next V-st, [ch 3, sl st in sp before next V-st, ch 3, (hdc, ch 1, join, ch 1, hdc) in ch-sp of next V-st] twice, fasten off.

Make 8 filler motifs in all.

Border

Rnd 1: Join yarn with sl st in ch-5 sp at one end of strip, ch 5 (counts as dc, ch 2), (dc, ch 2, V-st) in same ch-5 sp, *[sk next 4 sts, V-st in next st, (V-st, ch 2, V-st) in next ch-3 sp, sk next st, V-st in next st, (V-st, ch 2, V-st) in next ch-5 sp] twice, **sk next 4 sts, V-st in next st, V-st in center of motif joining, V-st in end of Row 2 of filler, V-st in center of Row 1 of filler, V-st in end of Row 2 of filler, V-st in center of motif joining, sk next st, V-st in next st, (V-st, ch 2, V-st) in next ch-5 sp; repeat from ** 3 more times, sk next 4 sts, V-st in next st, (V-st, ch 2, V-st) in next ch-3 sp, sk next st, V-st in next st***, (V-st, ch 2, V-st) in next ch-5 sp; repeat from * to ***, join with sl st in 3rd ch of beg ch-5.

Rnd 2: Sl st in ch-sp of first V-st, ch 3, 2 dc in same ch-sp, 3 dc in each ch-2 sp around, join with sl st in top of beg-ch.

Rnd 3: Ch 4 (counts as dc, ch 1), dc in same st as joining, sl st in next st, sk next st, *(dc, ch 1, dc) in sp before next st, sk next st, sl st in next st, sk next st; repeat from * around, join with sl st in 3rd ch of beg ch-4, fasten off.

Finishing

With a yarn needle, weave in ends. Immerse the piece in cool water, then squeeze out the excess water, taking care not to wring or twist. Place the piece on a towel on a flat surface and gently stretch to open up the lace pattern. Leave until completely dry.

Broomstick Lace

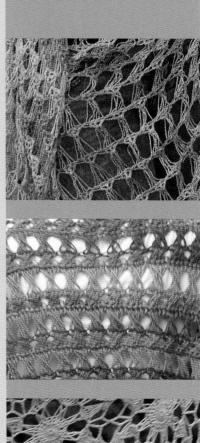

Broomstick lace dates back to the nineteenth century, probably originating in Europe. It has also been called jiffy lace, peacock eye crochet, witchcraft lace, and lattice loop (in Sweden). Its most common name comes from the fact that it was originally worked on the end of a broomstick. The larger the "broomstick" (or knitting needle, today), the more open and lacy the fabric will be. For a denser, more closely woven fabric, use a smaller knitting needle. A number of different knitting needles work well for broomstick lace—lightweight plastic needles, hand-carved wooden needles, and circular needles (which are two needle tips joined by a flexible plastic cable). Use whatever works best for you and the project you are working on.

Broomstick lace is made in two passes. In the first pass, loops are picked up across a row of crochet and placed on the broomstick needle. In the second pass, the loops are grouped and worked off of the needle. See page 89 for a step-by-step broomstick lace tutorial.

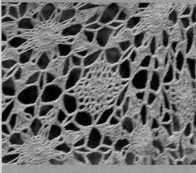

Ardeona Lace

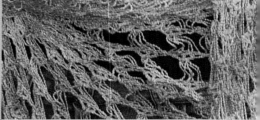

SKILL LEVEL

EASY

Vibrant shades of orange swirl and dance in this shimmery shawl. Very simple increases create a triangle shape that can be worn as a traditional shawl, folded over to wear as a scarf, wrapped around the neck as a cowl, or even clasped around the waist as a sarong!

Special Stitches

Beg-inc sh (Beginning increase shell): Holding loops together as one, insert hook under first 3 loops, yarn over and loosely pull up loop, ch 3 (counts as dc), 5 dc in same set of 3 loops, sliding loops off needle.

Inc sh (Increase shell): Holding loops together as one, 6 dc in indicated set of 3 loops, sliding loops off needle.

Sh (Shell): Holding loops together as one, 3 dc in indicated set of 3 loops, sliding loops off needle.

FINISHED SIZE

51 in./129.5 cm across by 91 in./231 cm long

YARN

Interlacements Rick Rack; (16 oz/454 g, 1200 yd./1097 m) hank:

1 hank Soliel

CROCHET HOOK

US H-8 (5mm) or size needed to obtain gauge.

US-50 (25mm) knitting needle (for broomstick lace)

ADDITIONAL MATERIALS

Yarn needle

GAUGE

3 shells in pattern = 4 in./10 cm; 4 rows = 3 in./7.5 cm

Instructions

Row 1: Ch 4 (beg ch counts as first dc), 5 dc in 4th ch from hook—6 dc.

Row 2: Work Broomstick Lace Row 1—6 loops on knitting needle.

Row 3: Beg-inc sh in first 3 loops (each inc sh counts as 2 regular shells), inc sh in last 3 loops—4 sh (12 dc).

Row 4: Work Broomstick Lace Row 1—12 loops on knitting needle.

Row 5: Beg-inc sh in first 3 loops, (sh in next 3 loops) up to last 3 loops, inc sh in last 3 loops—6 sh (18 dc).

Rows 6 and 7: Repeat Rows 4 and 5—8 sh (24 dc).

Row 8: Repeat Row 4—24 loops on knitting needle.

Row 9: Beg-inc sh in first 3 loops, inc sh in next 3 loops, (sh in next 3 loops) up to last 6 loops, (inc sh in next 3 loops) twice—12 sh (36 dc).

Rows 10–57: Repeat Rows 2–9 six times—72 sh (216 dc) at the end of Row 57.

Finishing

With a yarn needle, weave in ends. Immerse the piece in cool water, then squeeze out the excess water, taking care not to wring or twist. Place the piece on a towel on a flat surface and gently stretch to open up the lace pattern. Leave until completely dry.

NOTE Broomstick lace is worked with the RS facing at all times. Do not turn at end of broomstick lace rows.

Chianti

Flirty and fun, this little shrug is made all in one piece and then seamed at the shoulders. This is one of those pieces that looks great worn casual with jeans but looks equally cute dressed up with a little skirt and heels.

Special Stitches

Beg dc-cr (Beginning double crochet-cross): Sk next stitch, dc in next 2 stitches, working over stitches just made, dc in skipped stitch.

Beg dec loop-cr (Beginning decrease loop-cross): Slide first 4 loops off hook, sk first 2 loops, insert hook in 3rd and 4th loops, holding both loops together as one, yarn over and loosely pull up loop, ch 1, sc in same set of 2 loops, holding skipped loops together as one, sc in 2nd set of loops.

Beg loop-cr (Beginning loop-cross): Slide first 4 loops off hook, sk first 2 loops, insert hook in 3rd and 4th loops, holding both loops together as one, yarn over and loosely pull up loop, ch 1, 2 sc in same set of 2 loops, holding skipped loops together as one, 2 sc in 2nd set of loops.

Dc-cr (Double crochet-cross): Sk next 2 stitches, dc in next 2 stitches, working over stitches just made, dc in first skipped stitch, dc in 2nd skipped stitch.

Dec loop-cr (Decrease loop-cross): Slide next 4 loops off hook, sk first 2 loops, holding 3rd and 4th loops together as one, sc in both loops, holding both skipped loops together as one, sc in 2nd set of loops.

Loop-cr: Slide next 4 loops off hook, sk first 2 loops, holding third and fourth loops together as one, 2 sc in both loops, holding both skipped loops together as one, 2 sc in 2nd set of loops.

NOTES

1. Broomstick lace is worked with the RS facing at all times. Do not turn at end of broomstick lace rows.
2. This shawl is worked from the lower back edge up to the back neck. The piece is then divided at the neck and the right and left fronts are worked separately down to the lower front edge.
3. To assemble, the stitches of the last row of the right front are sewn to the corresponding stitches of Row 1 of the back. The same is done with the left front.

FINISHED SIZE

40 in./101.5 cm from cuff to cuff

YARN

Red Heart Boutique Unforgettable; (100% acrylic; 3.5 oz/100 g, 279 yd./256 m ball):

4 balls #3955 Winery

CROCHET HOOK

US J-10 (6 mm) or size needed to obtain gauge
US-50 (25 mm) knitting needle (for broomstick lace)

ADDITIONAL MATERIALS

Yarn needle

GAUGE

12 sts and 6 rows in pattern = 4 in./10 cm

Instructions

Back

Ch 121.

Row 1 (WS): Sc in 2nd ch from hook and each ch across—120 sc.

Row 2 (RS): Ch 3 (counts as first dc here and throughout), turn, beg dc-cr in next 3 sts, *dc-cr in next 4 sts; repeat from * across—30 cr.

Row 3 (RS): Work Broomstick Lace First Pass—120 loops on needle.

Row 4 (RS): Beg loop-cr in first 4 loops, *loop-cr in next 4 loops; repeat from * across—30 loop-cr.

Row 5 (WS): Repeat Row 2.

Row 6 (RS): Ch 1, turn, sc in each st across.

Rows 7 - 22: Repeat Rows 3–6 four times.

Rows 23 - 25: Repeat Rows 3–5.

Right Front

Row 1 (RS): Ch 1, turn, sc in first st, sc in next 59 sts, turn, leaving remaining sts unworked for Left Front—60 sc.

Rows 2–25: Repeat Rows 3–6 of back six times.

Row 26: Repeat Row 3 of back.

Neck Shaping

Row 1 (RS): Beg loop-cr in first 4 loops, *loop-cr in next 4 loops; repeat from * up to last 4 loops, dec loop-cr in last 4 loops—58 sc.

Row 2 (WS): Ch 3, turn, dc in next st, *dc-cr in next 4 sts; repeat from * across—2 dc, 14 dc-cr.

Row 3 (RS): Ch 1, turn, sc in each st up to last 4 sts, [sc2tog] 2 times—56 sc.

Row 4 (RS): Work Broomstick Lace First Pass.

Rows 5–16: Repeat Rows 1–4 three times.

Row 17: Repeat Row 1, fasten off—42 sc.

Left Front

Row 1: With RS facing, join yarn with sc in first unworked st on last row of back, sc in remaining 59 sts, turn—60 sc.

Rows 2–26: Repeat pattern for right front.

Neck Shaping

Row 1: Beg dec loop-cr in first 4 loops, *loop-cr in next 4 loops; repeat from * across—58 sc.

Row 2: Ch 3, beg dc-cr in next 3 sts, *dc-cr in next 4 sts; repeat from * up to last 2 sts, dc in last 2 sts—2 dc, 14 dc-cr.

Row 3: Ch 1, turn, [sc2tog] 2 times, sc in each st across—56 sc.

Row 4: Work Broomstick Lace First Pass.

Rows 5–16: Repeat Rows 1–4 three times.

Row 17: Repeat Row 1, fasten off–42 sc.

Assembly

Matching sts of Row 17 of right front neck shaping with bottom loops of Row 1 of back, sew shoulder seam. Repeat for second shoulder.

Finishing

With a yarn needle, weave in ends. Immerse the piece in cool water, then squeeze out the excess water, taking care not to wring or twist. Place the piece on a towel on a flat surface and gently stretch to open up the lace pattern. Leave until completely dry.

Chica Mala

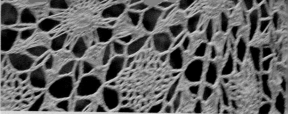

SKILL LEVEL

■■■■□

EXPERIENCED

Of course, you can work broomstick lace in the round—and here is the proof in this gorgeous, lacy wrap. Large circular motifs are created with broomstick lace and then assembled with a join-as-you go technique. Filler motifs are made last. The unusual broomstick-lace-in-the-round technique will have people wondering just how you made this showstopping piece!

FINISHED SIZE

31 in./78.5 cm wide by 72 in./183 cm long

YARN

Kollage Yarns Milky Whey; (50% Milk, 50% Soy; 1.76 oz/50 g, 137 yd./125 m hank):

9 hanks #7609 Mala Green

CROCHET HOOK

US H-8 (5 mm) or size needed to obtain gauge

US-50 (25 mm) circular knitting needle (for broomstick lace)

ADDITIONAL MATERIALS

Yarn needle

GAUGE

Motif = 10¼ in./26 cm

Special Technique

Broomstick Lace in the Round

Broomstick lace in the round, like flat broomstick lace, is made in two passes. In the first pass, loops are picked up around half the stitches of a round and placed on one end of the circular broomstick needle. Then the other end of the needle is introduced, pointed in the opposite direction. The remaining loops of same round are picked up and placed on the second half of the needle. In the second pass, the loops are grouped and worked off of the broomstick needle. See page 91 for a full step-by-step tutorial.

Special Stitches

Beg-lg sh (Beginning large shell): Holding loops together as one, insert hook under first 6 loops, yarn over and loosely draw up loop, ch 3 (counts as dc), (2 dc, ch 3, 3 dc) in same set of 6 loops, sliding loops off needle.

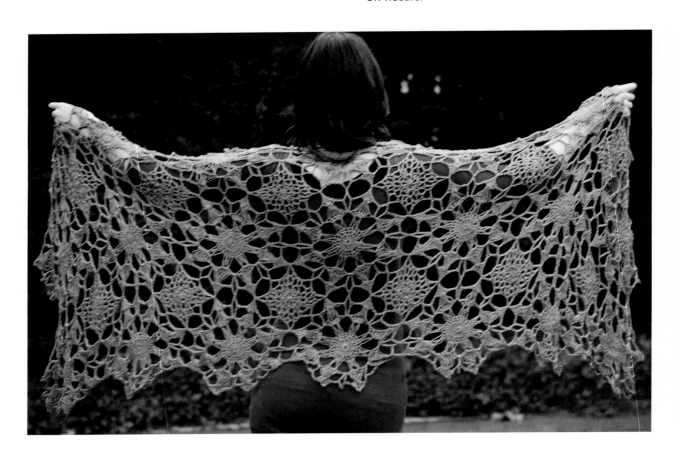

Beg-sh (Beginning shell): Holding loops together as one, insert hook under first 3 loops, yarn over and loosely draw up loop, ch 3 (counts as dc), 5 dc in same set of 3 loops, sliding loops off needle.

Join-sh (Join-shell): Holding next loops together as one, (3 dc, ch 1, motif-join, ch 1, 3 dc) in indicated set of 6 loops.

Lg sh (Large shell): Holding next loops together as one, (3 dc, ch 3, 3 dc) in indicated set of 6 loops.

Motif-join: Drop loop from hook, insert hook in center chain of corresponding chain-space, pick up dropped loop and pull through.

Sh (Shell): Holding loops together as one, 6 dc in indicated set of 3 loops, sliding loops off needle.

> **NOTES**
> 1. Broomstick lace is worked with the RS facing at all times. Do not turn at end of broomstick lace rows.
> 2. The shawl is made from 21 motifs joined into 3 rows of 7 motifs each. A join-as-you-go technique is used to join the motifs. Filler motifs are worked and joined later to fill in the opening between joined motifs.

Instructions

Strip 1 (motifs 1–7)

MOTIF 1

Ch 4, join with sl st to form ring.

Rnd 1: Ch 3 (counts as first dc here and throughout), 15 dc in ring, join with sl st in top of beg-ch—16 dc.

Rnd 2: Ch 3, 2 dc in next st, *dc in next st, 2 dc in next st; repeat from * around, join with sl st in top of beg-ch—24 dc.

Rnd 3: Work Broomstick Lace First Pass—24 loops on needle.

Rnd 4: Beg-sh in first 3 loops, ch 1, *sh in next 3 loops, ch 1; repeat from * around, join with sl st in top of beg-ch, ch 1, turn, sl st in next ch-1 sp, sl st in next st, turn—8 sh.

Rnd 5: Work Broomstick Lace First Pass—48 loops on needle.

Rnd 6: Beg-lg sh in first 6 loops, ch 2, (tr, ch 5, tr) in next ch-1 sp of Rnd 4, ch 2, *lg sh in next 6 loops, ch 2, (tr, ch 5, tr) in next ch-1 sp of Rnd 4, ch 2; repeat from * around, join with sl st in top of beg-ch, fasten off.

MOTIF 2

Work same as motif 1 through Rnd 5—48 loops on needle.

Hold motif 1 and motif 2 with WS together and stitches matching.

Rnd 6 (join to one previous motif): Beg-lg sh in first 6 loops, ch 2, (tr, ch 5, tr) in next ch-1 sp of Rnd 4; join motif 2 to motif 1 across one edge as follows: ch 2, join-sh in next 6 loops, ch 2, (tr, ch 2, motif-join, ch 2, tr) in next ch-1 sp of Rnd 4, ch 2, join-sh in next 6 loops; complete motif 2 as follows: ch 2, (tr, ch 5, tr) in next ch-1 sp of Rnd 4, ch 2, *lg sh in next 6 loops, ch 2, (tr, ch 5, tr) in next ch-1 sp of Rnd 4, ch 2; repeat from * around, join with sl st in top of beg-ch, fasten off.

MOTIFS 3–7

Work same as motif 2, joining each motif to previous motif to form a long strip.

Strip 2 (Motifs 8–14)

MOTIF 8

Work same as motif 2, joining motif 8 to motif 1 to begin next row of motifs.

MOTIF 9

Work same as motif 1 through Rnd 5—48 loops on needle.

Hold motif 9 and motif 8 with WS together and stitches matching.

Rnd 6: Beg-lg sh in first 6 loops, ch 2, (tr, ch 5, tr) in next ch-1 sp of Rnd 4; join motif 9 to motif 8 across one edge as follows: ch 2, join-sh in next 6 loops, ch 2, (tr, ch 2, motif-join, ch 2, tr) in next ch-1 sp of Rnd 4, ch 2, join-sh in next 6 loops; continue motif 9 only: ch 2, (tr, ch 5, tr) in next ch-1 sp of Rnd 4; hold motif 9 and motif 2 with WS together and sts matching, join motifs as follows: ch 2, join-sh in next 6 loops, ch 2, (tr, ch 2, motif-join, ch 2, tr) in next ch-1 sp of Rnd 4, ch 2, join-sh; complete motif 9 as follows: ch 2, (tr, ch 5, tr) in next ch-1 sp of Rnd 4, ch 2, *lg sh in next 6 loops, ch 2, (tr, ch 5, tr) in next ch-1 sp of Rnd 4, ch 2; repeat from * around, join with sl st in top of beg-ch, fasten off.

MOTIFS 10–14

Work same as motif 9, joining each motif to previous motif and next motif of Strip 1.

Strip 3 (Motifs 15–22)

Work and join same as Strip 2, joining to Strip 2.

Filler Motifs (make and join 12)

Ch 3, join with sl st to form ring.

Rnd 1: Ch 4 (counts as dc, ch 1), (dc in ring, ch 1) 7 times, join with sl st in 3rd ch of beg ch-4 – 8 dc, 8 ch-1 sps.

Rnd 2: Sl st in next ch-1 sp, ch 2 (counts as hdc), (2 hdc, ch 3, 2 hdc) in next ch-1 sp, *hdc in next ch-1 sp, (2 hdc, ch 3, 2 hdc) in next ch-1 sp; repeat from * around, join with sl st in top of beg-ch – 20 hdc.

Rnd 3: Ch 5 (counts as hdc, ch 3), hdc in same st as join, [hdc, (ch 3, hdc) 3 times] in next ch-3 sp, *sk next 2 sts, (hdc, ch 3, hdc) in next st, [hdc, (ch 3, hdc) 3 times] in next ch-3 sp; repeat from * around, join with a sl st in 2nd ch of beg ch-5 – 24 hdc.

Hold filler motif in an opening between joined motifs.

Rnd 4 (joining rnd): (Ch 5, motif-join to any ch-5 sp in edge of opening, ch 2, dc) in first ch-3 sp of filler, sc in next ch-3 sp, (dc, ch 2, motif-join to center of next motif joining of opening, ch 2, dc) in next ch-3 sp of filler, sc in next ch-3 sp, *(dc, ch 2, motif-join in next ch-5 sp in edge of opening, ch 2, dc) in next ch-3 sp of filler, sc in next ch-3 sp; repeat from * around, join with sl st in 3rd ch of beg ch-5, fasten off.

Finishing

With a yarn needle, weave in ends. Immerse the piece in cool water, then squeeze out the excess water, taking care not to wring or twist. Place the piece on a towel on a flat surface and gently stretch to open up the lace pattern. Leave until completely dry.

Tunisian Crochet

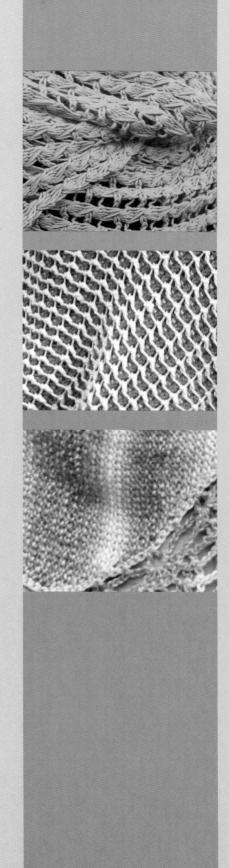

Also known as afghan stitch, hook knitting, tricot crochet, shepherd's knitting, and railroad knitting, Tunisian crochet uses a long hook, sometimes with a cable attached to the end to provide enough room for all the stitches. Tunisian crochet is worked in two steps. The first pass (forward pass) of each row is worked from right to left, keeping all the loops on the hook. The second pass (return pass) is worked from left to right, removing each loop from the hook. There is no turning while working Tunisian crochet. This technique is a cross between knitting and crochet. Full step-by-step instructions can be found on page 93.

Clementine Shells

SKILL LEVEL

EASY

Tunisian crochet is often worked in such a way that it creates a dense fabric, similar to a knitted fabric. But it also can create a beautiful, open pattern like the one in this shawl. Very simple and relaxing, this is one of those great projects to work on while watching a movie. Nobody but you ever need know that, though, since the simple pattern produces such an elegant piece.

FINISHED SIZE

13 in./33 cm wide by 86 in./218.5 cm long.

YARN

Knit Picks Shine Sport; (60% Pima Cotton, 40% Modal Natural Beech Wood Fiber; 1.76 oz/50 g, 110 yd./101 m ball):

9 balls Clementine

CROCHET HOOK

US K-10 1/2 (6.5mm) Tunisian hook

ADDITIONAL MATERIALS

Yarn needle

GAUGE

4 shells in pattern = 4 in./10 cm; 5 rows = 4½in./ 11. 5cm

Special Stitches

Beg-sh (Beginning shell): Ch 2, work 4 Tdc in indicated 5 vertical bars at the same time.

Sh (Shell): Work 5 Tdc in indicated 5 vertical bars at the same time.

Tdc (Tunisian double-crochet): Yarn over, insert hook in indicated space, pull up a loop, yarn over, draw through 2 loops on hook.

> **NOTES**
> 1. Tunisian crochet has a tendency to "lean" to the right. This is easily corrected by wet blocking.
> 2. When instructed to work into two or more vertical bars "at the same time," insert the hook under all of the vertical bars and work as if working into a single stitch.

Instructions

Ch 51.

Row 1: Forward Pass: [Yarn over, insert hook in 3rd ch from hook, draw up a loop, yarn over, pull through 2 loops on hook] 4 times, *sk next 3 chs, 5 Tdc in next ch; repeat from * across—65 Tdc. **Return Pass:** Working from left to right, yarn over and draw through first 5 loops on hook, *ch 4, draw through next 5 loops on hook; repeat from * across.

Row 2: Forward Pass: Beg-sh in first 5 vertical bars, *Sh in next 5 vertical bars; repeat from * across. **Return Pass:** Work same as Row 1 Return pass—13 shells.

Rows 3–95: Repeat Row 2 ninety-three times or to desired length.

Finishing

With a yarn needle, weave in ends. Immerse the piece in cool water, then squeeze out the excess water, taking care not to wring or twist. Place the piece on a towel on a flat surface and gently stretch to open up the lace pattern. Leave until completely dry.

Cascading Rivers

SKILL LEVEL

■■■◻
INTERMEDIATE

You will be so pleased with the unique fabric that is produced with this pattern! Little white "boxes" frame the green stitches, creating almost a plaid look. This is a versatile piece that can be worn in many different ways.

FINISHED SIZE

24 in./61 cm wide including edging by 64 in./
162.5 cm long

YARN

Knit Picks Brava Worsted; (100% Premium Acrylic;
3.5 oz/100 g, 218 yd./199 m ball):

3 balls Tidepool (A)

3 balls Cream (B)

CROCHET HOOK

US K-10½ (6.5 mm) or size needed to obtain gauge

US M/N-13 (9 mm) Tunisian crochet hook

ADDITIONAL MATERIALS

Yarn needle

GAUGE

7 Tdc and 6 ch-1 sps = 4 in./10 cm; 8 rows in pattern
= 4 in./10 cm

Special Stitches

BPdc (Back-post double crochet): Yarn over, insert hook
from back to front and then to back again around
both posts of st in prev row (when it is a dc2tog,
go around both posts), yarn over and draw up loop,
[yarn over and draw through 2 loops on hook] twice.

Dc2tog (Double crochet 2 together): [Yarn over, insert
hook in next stitch and draw up a loop, yarn over and
draw through 2 loops on hook] twice, yarn over and
draw through all 3 loops on hook.

FPdc (Front-post double crochet): Yarn over, insert
hook from front to back and then to front again
around post of st in prev row (when it is a dc2tog,
go around both posts), yarn over and draw up loop,
[yarn over and draw through 2 loops on hook] twice.

Tdc (Tunisian double-crochet): Yarn over, insert hook
in indicated space, draw up a loop, yarn over, draw
through 2 loops on hook.

Tss (Tunisian simple stitch): Working from right to left,
insert hook in next chain, yarn over and draw up a
loop.

> **NOTE** The body of the wrap is made with a
> Tunisian hook; the edging and collar are made
> using a regular crochet hook.

Instructions

With Tunisian Hook and A, ch 65.

Row 1: Forward Pass: Tss in 2nd ch from hook and each
ch across—65 loops on hook. **Return Pass:** With B,
yarn over and draw through first loop on hook, *yarn
over and draw through 2 loops on hook, repeat from
* across.

Row 2: Forward Pass: With B, ch 3 (counts as first Tdc,
ch 1), sk next vertical bar, Tdc in next vertical bar, *ch
1, sk next vertical bar, Tdc in next vertical bar; repeat
from * across. **Return Pass:** With A, work same as
Row 1 Return Pass.

Row 4: Forward Pass: With B, *Working behind previous row in skipped vertical bars 3 rows below (i.e. in Row 1) , *Tdc in next skipped vertical bar, Tss in next vertical bar of current row; repeat from * across. **Return Pass:** With A, work same as Row 1 Return Pass.

Repeat Rows 3 and 4 until piece measures approximately 56 in. (142 cm) long.

Change to standard crochet hook and work with standard crochet hook for remainder of piece.

Last Row: Ch 1, sc in first vertical bar *sc in next ch-2 sp, sc in next vertical bar; repeat from * across, do not turn or fasten off.

Bottom Edging

Row 1: Ch 1, pivot to work in ends of rows across side edge, working over carried strands (to hide them), sc in end of first row, 2 sc in end of each row up to last row, sc in last row, fasten off.

Top Edging

Working in ends of rows across opposite side, working over carried strands, 2 sc in end of each row up to last row, sc in end of last row, fasten off leaving a long length for sewing.

Assembly

Fold piece in half, bringing first and last row together and matching up stitches of (folded) top edging, sew first 60 sts together, leave remaining sts unsewn for neck opening.

Collar

Rnd 1: Join A with sl st in center of seam at neck opening, ch 3 (counts as dc), *dc2tog; repeat from * around, join with sl st in top of beg-ch.

Rnds 2 and 3: Ch 2 (counts as hdc), *FPdc around next st, BPdc around next st; repeat from * around, join with sl st in top of beg-ch. Fasten off after last rnd.

Finishing

With a yarn needle, weave in ends.

Row 3: Forward Pass: With A, ch 3 (counts as first Tdc, ch 1), working in vertical bars 2 rows (in Row 1) below, sk next vertical bar, Tdc in next vertical bar, *ch 1, sk next vertical bar, Tdc in next vertical bar; repeat from * across. **Return Pass:** With B, working from left to right, yarn over and draw through first loop on hook, *ch 2, draw through next loop on hook; repeat from * across.

Water Lily

SKILL LEVEL

EXPERIENCED

Wrap yourself in this flattering, cozy shawl done in Tunisian crochet with a pineapple border in traditional crochet stitches. Subtle shaping is achieved through increasing at the end of each forward pass row on the first part of the shawl, working even across the back, then decreasing at the end of each forward pass row in the last section.

FINISHED SIZE

16½ in./42 cm at widest section (not including border); 54 in./137 cm from point to point; border 7 in./18 cm wide

YARN

RED HEART Boutique Treasure: (70% Acrylic, 30% Wool; 3.50 oz/100 g, 151 yd./138 m ball): 4 balls #1919 Watercolors

CROCHET HOOK

US K-10½ (6.5 mm) or size needed to obtain gauge
US M/N-13 (9 mm) afghan hook

ADDITIONAL MATERIALS

Yarn needle

GAUGE

12 Tdc and 10 rows = 4 in./10 cm

Special Stitches

Beg-sh (Beginning shell): (Sl st, ch 3, dc, ch 2, 2 dc) in indicated space.

Sh (Shell): (2 dc, ch 2, 2 dc) in indicated space.

Tdc (Tunisian double-crochet): Yarn over, insert hook in indicated space, draw up a loop, yarn over, draw through 2 loops on hook.

NOTES

1. The body of the wrap is made with a Tunisian hook; the border is made using a regular crochet hook.
2. The body of the wrap is worked side to side, from side point to side point.
3. When instructed to work into two or more vertical bars "at the same time," insert the hook under all of the vertical bars and work as if working into a single stitch.

Instructions

Row 1 (RS): Forward Pass: Ch 3, Tdc in 3rd ch from hook—2 loops on hook. **Return Pass:** Working from left to right, yarn over and draw through first loop on hook, *yarn over, draw through 2 loops on hook, repeat from * across.

Row 2: Forward Pass: Ch 2, 2 Tdc in next vertical bar—3 loops on hook. **Return Pass:** Work same as Row 1 Return Pass.

Row 3: Forward Pass: Ch 2, Tdc in each vertical bar up to last bar, 2 Tdc in last vertical bar—4 loops on hook. **Return Pass:** Work same as Row 1 Return Pass.

Rows 4–49: Repeat Row 3 forty-six times—50 loops on hook at end of Row 49.

Rows 50–92: Forward Pass: Ch 2, Tdc in each vertical bar across. **Return Pass:** Work same as Row 1 Return Pass.

Rows 93–140: Forward Pass: Ch 2, Tdc in each vertical bar up to last 2 bars, Tdc in next 2 vertical bars at the same time—one less loop on hook at end of each row, 2 loops remain at end of Row 140 Forward Pass. **Return Pass:** Work same as Row 1 Return Pass.

Row 141: Forward Pass: Ch 2, Tdc in next vertical bar— 2 loops on hook. **Return Pass:** Yarn over and draw through both loops on hook.

Border

Row 1: Ch 1, working in ends of rows across diagonal sides and bottom with regular hook, work 193 sc evenly spaced across, turn.

Row 2: Ch 5 (counts as dc, ch 2), dc in first sc, *ch 3, sk next 3 sts, sc in next st, ch 3, sk next 3 sts, (dc, ch 2, dc) in next st; repeat from * across, turn—50 dc, 24 sc.

Row 3: Beg-sh in first ch-2 sp, ch 3, *[tr, (ch 1, tr) 5 times] in next ch-2 sp, ch 3, sh in next ch-2 sp; repeat from * across, turn—13 sh, 72 tr.

Row 4: Sl st in each st to first ch-2 sp, beg-sh in first ch-2 sp, *ch 3, sk next ch-3 sp, (sc in next tr, ch 3) 6 times, sh in ch-2 sp of next sh; repeat from * across, turn— 13 sh, 72 sc.

Row 5: Sl st in each st to first ch-2 sp, beg-sh in first ch-2 sp, *ch 3, sk next ch-3 sp, (sc in next ch-3 sp, ch 3) 5 times, sh in ch-2 sp of next sh; repeat from * across, turn—13 sh, 60 sc.

Row 6: Sl st in each st to first ch-2 sp, beg-sh in first ch-2 sp, *ch 3, sk next ch-3 sp, (sc in next ch-3 sp, ch 3) 4 times, sh in ch-2 sp of next sh; repeat from * across, turn—13 sh, 48 sc.

Row 7: Sl st in each st to first ch-2 sp, beg-sh in first ch-2 sp, *ch 5, sk next ch-3 sp, sc in next ch-3 sp, (ch 3, sc in next ch-3 sp) twice, ch 5, sh in ch-2 sp of next sh; repeat from * across, turn—13 sh, 36 sc.

Row 8: Sl st in each st to first ch-2 sp, (sl st, ch 3, 2 dc, ch 3, 3 dc) in first ch-2 sp, *ch 5, sc in next ch-3 sp, ch 3, sc in next ch-3 sp, ch 5, (3 dc, ch 3, 3 dc) in ch-2 sp of next sh; repeat from * across, fasten off—78 dc, 24 sc.

Finishing

With a yarn needle, weave in ends. Immerse the piece in cool water, then squeeze out the excess water, taking care not to wring or twist. Place the piece on a towel on a flat surface and gently stretch to open up the lace pattern. Leave until completely dry.

Double-Ended Crochet

This technique is a variation of Tunisian crochet in which the work is turned; it uses multiple yarns and a long needle with hooks on each end. Like Tunisian crochet, each row has two parts. The forward pass, in which you pick up the loops, is worked from right to left. All the loops are then pushed to the opposite end of the hook, the piece is turned, and a second yarn is used to remove the loops from the hook in the return pass. Developed by Mary Middleton in the 1970s, it is also known as crochet on the double, cro-hook, and crochenit. It's a lovely cross between knitting and crochet that creates a colorful, reversible fabric. See page 96 for a step-by-step tutorial.

Zen Garden

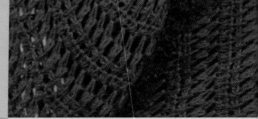

SKILL LEVEL

EASY

Wrap yourself in luxury with this long, dramatic shawl. The perfect beginner project for practicing double-ended crochet, it can be made as long or as short as you want. The edging is added last, using traditional crochet.

FINISHED SIZE

15½ in./39.5 cm wide by 74 in./188 cm long

YARN

Cascade Yarns Pure Alpaca; (100% Baby Alpaca;
3.50 oz/100 g, 220 yd./200 m ball):

2 balls #3043 African Violet (A)

2 balls #3047 Chianti Heather (B)

1 ball #3001 Black (C)

SKILL LEVEL

Easy

CROCHET HOOK

US-I/9 (5.5 mm) double-ended hook

ADDITIONAL MATERIALS

Yarn needle

GAUGE

14 Tdc and 5 rows = 4 in./10 cm

Special Stitches

Cross: Sk next stitch, dc in next stitch, working in front
of stitch just made, dc in skipped stitch.

Tdc (Tunisian double crochet): Working from right to
left, yarn over, insert hook in indicated chain or space,
yarn over and draw up a loop, yarn over and draw
through 2 loops on hook.

NOTES

1. The body of the wrap is made using the double-
ended hook; a regular crochet hook is used for
the edging and the border.

2. When a color is not in use, it is dropped and
loosely carried up side of work when needed
again.

3. When instructed to work into two or more
vertical bars "at the same time," insert the
hook under all of the vertical bars and work
as if working into a single stitch.

Instructions

With A, very *loosely* ch 57.

Row 1: Forward Pass: Tdc in 3rd ch from hook (beg ch
counts as first Tdc) and in each ch across, slide all
loops to opposite end of hook, turn—56 loops on
hook. **Return Pass:** With B, yarn over, draw through
first 2 loops on hook, *ch 2, draw through next 2
loops on hook; repeat from * across, do not turn.

Row 2: Forward Pass: With B, ch 2 (counts as first Tdc
here and throughout), Tdc in next 2 vertical bars at
the same time, *2 Tdc in next 2 vertical bars at the
same time; repeat from * across, slide all loops to
opposite end of hook, turn. **Return Pass:** With A,
draw through first 2 loops on hook, ch 2, *draw
through next 2 loops, ch 2; repeat from * across,
do not turn.

Row 3: Forward Pass: With A, *2 Tdc in next ch-2 sp; repeat from * across, Tdc in last 2 vertical bars at the same time, slide all loops to opposite end of hook, turn. **Return Pass:** With B, work same as Row 2 Return Pass.

Rows 4–89: Repeat Rows 2 and 3 forty-three times.

Row 90: Repeat Row 2.

Last Row: Ch 2, *2 hdc in next ch-2 sp; repeat from * across, hdc in last 2 vertical bars at the same time, fasten off.

Edging

Row 1: Working in ends of rows across one long edge, join C with sl st in end of Row 1, ch 3 (counts as dc), dc in same sp, *ch 1, 2 dc in end of next row; repeat from * across, turn.

Row 2: Ch 3, dc in next st, *cross over next 2 sts; repeat from * across, fasten off.

Repeat across second long edge.

Finishing

With a yarn needle, weave in ends. Immerse the piece in cool water, then squeeze out the excess water, taking care not to wring or twist. Place the piece on a towel on a flat surface and gently stretch to open up the lace pattern. Leave until completely dry.

Sophisticated Lady

SKILL LEVEL

■■■▭
INTERMEDIATE

Worked vertically, with tall, open stitches, this wrap can easily be altered to any desired length. A longer length allows you to wrap it around multiple times, draping the wrap over each shoulder and leaving the rest to hang down the back. You can achieve many different looks with this graceful piece—experiment and have fun!

FINISHED SIZE

12½ in./32 cm wide by 72 in./183 cm long, plus
5 in./12.5 cm border

YARN

Bernat Sheep(ish) by Vickie Howell (70% Acrylic/
30% Wool; 3 oz/85 g, 167 yd./153 m);

2 balls #0003 Grey(ish) (A)

2 balls #0005 Plum(ish) (B)

1 ball #0002 Gun Metal(ish) (C)

CROCHET HOOK

US I-9 (5.5 mm) or size to obtain gauge

13 in./33 cm double-ended crochet hook

ADDITIONAL MATERIALS

Yarn needle

GAUGE

7 Tdc and 6 ch-2 sps in pattern = 4 in./10 cm; 6 rows
= 6 in./15 cm

Special Stitches

Cl (Cluster): Yarn over, insert hook in indicated stitch and
draw up a loop, yarn over and draw through 2 loops
on hook (2 loops remain on hook); [yarn over, insert
hook in *same* stitch and draw up a loop, yarn over
and draw through 2 loops on hook] 2 times; yarn
over and draw through all 4 loops on hook.

Tdc (Tunisian double crochet): Working from right to
left, yarn over, insert hook in indicated chain or space,
yarn over and draw up a loop, yarn over and draw
through 2 loops on hook.

NOTES

1. The body of the wrap is made using a double-
ended hook. A regular crochet hook is used for
the edging and border.

2. Color A is dropped when not in use and loosely
carried up side of work as needed. All other
colors are fastened off after use.

3. When instructed to work into two or more
vertical bars "at the same time," insert the
hook under all of the vertical bars and work
as if working into a single stitch.

Instructions

With A, ch 64.

Row 1 (RS): Forward Pass: Tdc in 7th ch from hook (beg ch counts as 2 base ch, first Tdc, and one ch-2 sp), *ch 2, sk next 2 ch, Tdc in next ch; repeat from * across, push all loops to opposite end of hook, turn—21 loops on hook. **Return Pass:** With B, yarn over and draw through first loop on hook, *ch 3, draw through next loop on hook; repeat from * across, do not turn.

Row 2: Forward Pass: With B, ch 2 (counts as first Tdc here and throughout), 2 Tdc under first vertical bar, 3 Tdc under next vertical bar and each vertical bar across, push all loops to opposite end of hook, turn, fasten off B—63 loops on hook. **Return Pass:** With A, yarn over and draw through first 3 loops on hook, *ch 2, draw through next 3 loops on hook; repeat from * across, do not turn.

Row 3: Forward Pass: With A, ch 4 (counts as Tdc, ch 2 here and throughout), Tdc under next 3 vertical bars at the same time, *ch 2, Tdc under next 3 vertical bars at same time; repeat from * across, push all loops to opposite end of hook, turn. **Return Pass:** With C, work same as Row 1 Return Pass.

Row 4: Forward Pass: With C, ch 2, Tdc in first vertical bar, *Tdc in next ch-3 sp, Tdc in next vertical bar; repeat from * across, push all loops to opposite end of hook, turn, fasten off C—41 loops on hook. **Return Pass:** With A, work same as Row 1 Return Pass.

Row 5: Forward Pass: With A, ch 4, sk next vertical bar, Tdc in next vertical bar, *ch 2, sk next vertical bar, Tdc in next vertical bar; repeat from * across, push all loops to opposite end of hook, turn—21 loops on hook. **Return Pass:** With B, work same as Row 1 Return Pass.

Rows 6–65: Repeat Rows 2–5 fifteen times or to desired length.

Row 66: Repeat Row 2.

Last Row: With A, ch 4, dc under next 3 vertical bars at the same time, *ch 2, dc under next 3 vertical bars at the same time; repeat from * across, fasten off.

Top Edging

Row 1: With RS facing, working in ends of rows, join B with sl st in end of first row, ch 3 (counts as dc), dc in end of same row, *ch 1, 2 dc in end of next row: repeat from * across, turn—134 dc and 66 ch-1 sps.

Row 2: Ch 1, sc in first 2 sts, *sc in next ch-1 sp, sc in next 2 sts; repeat from * across, fasten off—200 sc.

Bottom Border

Row 1: Repeat Row 1 of top edging—134 dc and 66 ch-1 sps.

Row 2: Ch 1, sc in each st and sp across, evenly spacing 4 additional sc sts, turn—204 sc.

Row 3: Ch 8 (counts as dc, ch 5), sk next 6 sts, dc in next st, *ch 5, sk next 6 sts, dc in next st; repeat from * across, turn—30 dc, 29 ch-5 sps.

Row 4: Ch 6 (counts as dc, ch 3), cl in first dc, *sk next ch-3 sp, (cl, ch 5, cl) in next dc; repeat from * across to turning ch, sk next 5 ch, (cl, ch 3, dc) in next ch of turning ch—58 cl.

Row 5: Ch 1, sc in first st, sk next ch-3 sp, *ch 7, sc in next ch-5 sp; repeat from * across to turning ch, ch 7, sc in 3rd of turning ch—30 sc, 29 ch-7 sp.

Row 6: Ch 1, sc in first st, *9 sc in next ch-7 sp, sc in next st; repeat from * across, fasten off—291 sc.

Finishing

With a yarn needle, weave in ends. Immerse the piece in cool water, then squeeze out the excess water, taking care not to wring or twist. Place the piece on a towel on a flat surface and gently stretch to open up the lace pattern. Leave until completely dry.

Autumn Harvest

SKILL LEVEL

◼◼◼▭
EXPERIENCED

You can almost smell the pumpkin spice in this casual wrap. Made in the colors of falling leaves, this is a perfect piece to throw over your shoulders on cool autumn nights. It works up very quickly, using a large hook and repetitive stitches.

FINISHED SIZE

53 in./134.5 cm across front; 40 in./101.5 cm from front to center of back

YARN

Berroco Comfort Chunky; (50% Super Fine Nylon, 50% Super Fine Acrylic; 3.50 oz/100 g, 150 yd./ 138 m) skein:

2 balls #5745 Filbert (A)

2 balls #5724 Pumpkin (B)

2 balls #5703 Barley (C)

2 balls #5752 Adirondack (D)

CROCHET HOOKS

US-M/N-13 (9 mm) or size to obtain gauge

24 in./60 cm M/N-13 (9 mm) circular Tunisian crochet hook

ADDITIONAL MATERIALS

Yarn needle

GAUGE

In pattern using circular Tunisian crochet hook, 12 sts and 8 rows = 4 in./10 cm

Special Stitch

Tdc (Tunisian double crochet): Working from right to left, yarn over, insert hook in indicated space, yarn over and draw up a loop, yarn over and draw through 2 loops on hook.

> **NOTES**
> 1. Each color is dropped when not in use and loosely carried up the side of the work when needed again.
> 2. When instructed to work into 2 or more vertical bars "at the same time," insert the hook under all of the vertical bars and work as if working into a single stitch.
> 3. Sometimes you will be instructed to "ch 2 and draw through 2 loops on hook." This means you should draw the first loop on the hook (at head of hook) through the next 2 loops on the hook. Do not work a yarn over before drawing through the next 2 loops.

Instructions

Back

With A, ch 3.

Row 1: Forward Pass: 5 Tdc in 3rd ch from hook (beg ch counts as first Tdc), push all loops to opposite end of hook, turn—6 loops on hook. **Return Pass:** With B, working from left to right, yarn over and draw through first loop, *ch 2 and draw through 2 loops on hook; repeat from * up to last loop, ch 2, draw through last loop.

Row 2: Forward Pass: With B, working from right to left, ch 2 (counts as first Tdc here and throughout), 2 Tdc in first vertical bar, *2 Tdc in next 2 vertical bars at the same time; repeat from * up to last vertical bar, 3 Tdc in last vertical bar, push all loops to opposite end of hook, drop color, turn—10 loops on hook. **Return Pass:** With C, work same as Row 1 Return Pass.

Row 3: Forward Pass: With C, work same as Row 2 Forward Pass—14 loops on hook. **Return Pass:** With D, work same as Row 1 Return Pass.

Row 4: Forward Pass: With D, work same as Row 2 Forward Pass—18 loops on hook. **Return Pass:** With A, work same as Row 1 Return Pass.

Row 5: Forward Pass: With A, work same as Row 2 Forward Pass—22 loops on hook. **Return Pass:** With B, work same as Row 1 Return Pass.

Rows 6–25: Repeat Rows 2–5 five times—102 loops on hook at end of Row 25 Forward Pass.

Row 26: Repeat Row 2—106 loops on hook at end of forward pass.

Fasten off B and D.

First Front

Row 1: Forward Pass: With C, working from right to left, ch 2, 2 Tdc in first vertical bar, *2 Tdc in next 2 vertical bars at the same time; repeat from * 24 more times, push all loops to opposite end of hook, leaving remaining sts unworked, turn—53 loops on hook. **Return Pass:** With D, working from left to right, yarn over and draw through first loop, *ch 2 and draw through 2 loops on hook; repeat from * up to last loop, ch 2, draw through last loop.

Row 2: Forward Pass: With D, working from right to left, ch 2, *2 Tdc in next 2 vertical bars at the same time; repeat from * up to last vertical bar, 3 Tdc in last vertical bar, push all loops to opposite end of hook, drop color, turn—55 loops on hook. **Return Pass:** With A, work same as Row 1 Return Pass.

Row 3: Forward Pass: With A, working from right to left, ch 2, 2 Tdc in first vertical bar, *2 Tdc in next 2 vertical bars at the same time; repeat from * up to last vertical bar, Tdc in last vertical bar, push all loops to opposite end of hook, drop color, turn—57 loops on hook. **Return Pass:** With B, work same as Row 1 Return Pass.

Row 4: Forward Pass: With B, work same as Row 2 Forward Pass—59 loops on hook. **Return Pass:** With C, work same as Row 1 Return Pass.

Row 5: Forward Pass: With C, work same as Row 3 Forward Pass—61 loops on hook. **Return Pass:** With D, work same as Row 1 Return Pass.

Rows 6–9: Repeat Rows 2–5—69 loops on hook at end of Row 9 Forward Pass.

Row 10: Repeat Row 2—71 loops on hook at end of forward pass.

Row 11: Forward Pass: With A, working from right to left, ch 2, *2 Tdc in next 2 vertical bars at the same time; repeat from * up to last vertical bar, Tdc in last vertical bar, push all loops to opposite end of hook, drop color, turn. **Return Pass:** With B, work same as Row 1 Return Pass.

Row 12: Forward Pass: With B, work same as Row 11 Forward Pass. **Return Pass:** With C, work same as Row 1 Return Pass.

Row 13: Forward Pass: With C, work same as Row 11 Forward Pass. **Return Pass:** With D, work same as Row 1 Return Pass.

Last Row: Ch 2, *2 hdc in next 2 vertical bars at the same time; repeat from * up to last vertical bar, hdc in last vertical bar, fasten off.

Second Front

Row 1: Forward Pass: With C, working from right to left, sk next 4 vertical bars on last row of back, join C with slip st in next 2 vertical bars at same time, ch 2, *2 Tdc in next 2 vertical bars at the same time; repeat from * up to last vertical bar, 3 Tdc in last vertical bar, push all loops to opposite end of hook, turn—53 loops on hook. **Return Pass:** With D, working from left to right, yarn over and draw through first loop, *ch 2 and draw through 2 loops on hook; repeat from * up to last loop, ch 2, draw through last loop.

Row 2: Forward Pass: With D, working from right to left, ch 2, 2 Tdc in first vertical bar, *2 Tdc in next 2 vertical bars at the same time; repeat from * up to last vertical bar, Tdc in last vertical bar, push all loops to opposite end of hook, drop color, turn—55 loops on hook. **Return Pass:** With A, work same as Row 1 Return Pass.

Row 3: Forward Pass: With A, working from right to left, ch 2, *2 Tdc in next 2 vertical bars at the same time; repeat from * up to last vertical bar, 3 Tdc in last vertical bar, push all loops to opposite end of hook, drop color, turn—57 loops on hook. **Return Pass:** With B, work same as Row 1 Return Pass.

Row 4: Forward Pass: With B, work same as Row 2 Forward Pass—59 loops on hook. **Return Pass:** With C, work same as Row 1 Return Pass.

Row 5: Forward Pass: With C, work same as Row 3 Forward Pass—61 loops on hook. **Return Pass:** With D, work same as Row 1 Return Pass.

Rows 6–9: Repeat Rows 2–5—69 loops on hook at end of Row 9 Forward Pass.

Row 10: Repeat Row 2—71 loops on hook at end of forward pass.

Row 11: Forward Pass: With A, working from right to left, ch 2, *2 Tdc in next 2 vertical bars at the same time; repeat from * up to last vertical bar, Tdc in last vertical bar, push all loops to opposite end of hook, drop color, turn. **Return Pass:** With B, work same as Row 1 Return Pass.

Row 12: Forward Pass: With B, work same as Row 11 Forward Pass. **Return Pass:** With C, work same as Row 1 Return Pass.

Row 13: Forward Pass: With C, work same as Row 11 Forward Pass. **Return Pass:** With D, work same as Row 1 Return Pass.

Last Row: Ch 2, *2 hdc in next 2 vertical bars at the same time; repeat from * up to last vertical bar, hdc in last vertical bar, do not fasten off.

Inside Front Border and Neck Shaping

Row 1: Ch 1, pivot to work in ends of rows around inside of fronts, working over carried strands (to hide them), 2 sc in end of each row to neck, sc evenly spaced across back neck edge, 2 sc in end of each row across second front, fasten off.

Outside Border

Row 1: Working in ends of rows around outside edge of wrap, working over carried strands, join D with sc in last row of one front, sc in same sp, 2 sc in end of each row to back point, 3 dc in bottom of Row 1 of back, 2 sc in end of each row up opposite side, fasten off.

Finishing

With a yarn needle, weave in ends.

Essential Crochet Techniques

Traditional Crochet Stitches

Single Crochet (sc)

Insert hook under both loops of the indicated stitch or through the indicated space; yarn over and pull up a loop through the stitch or space.

You will now have 2 loops on the hook.

Yarn over and pull through both loops on hook.

Single crochet made.

Half Double Crochet (hdc)

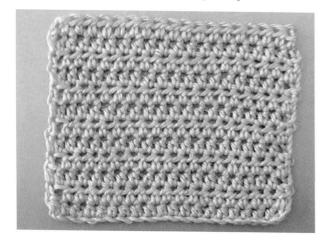

You will now have 3 loops on the hook.

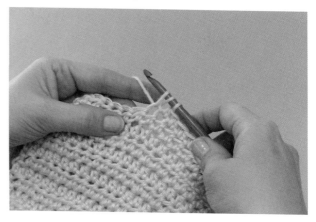

Yarn over, then insert hook in indicated stitch or space.

Yarn over hook and pull through all 3 loops on hook.

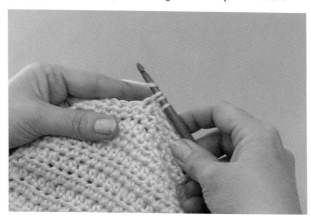

Yarn over and pull through stitch or space.

Half double crochet made.

Double Crochet (dc)

Yarn over, then insert hook in indicated stitch or space.

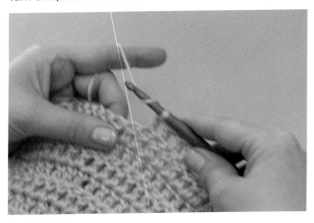

Yarn over, then pull through stitch or space.

You will now have 3 loops on the hook.

Yarn over and pull through 2 loops.

You will now have 2 loops on the hook.

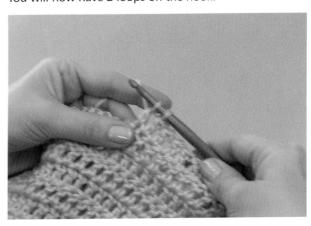

Yarn over and pull through remaining 2 loops.

Double crochet made.

Treble Crochet (tr)

You will now have 4 loops on the hook.

Yarn over 2 times, then insert hook in indicated stitch or space.

Yarn over and pull through 2 loops.

Yarn over, then pull through stitch or space.

You will now have 3 loops on the hook.

Yarn over and pull through next 2 loops on hook.

You will now have 2 loops on the hook.

Yarn over and pull through last 2 loops remaining on hook.

Treble crochet made.

Join-As-You-Go Technique

There are many variations to this technique but the basic concept is the same for each one. In this example, I will show you how to use a ch-3 join to join a small motif to the opening created by the joining of 4 large motifs.

The starting point:

Ch 1.

Remove the hook from the loop. Insert the hook in the center chain of the corresponding chain space you are joining to.

Insert hook back into the dropped loop.

Ch 1. Work next stitch of pattern as indicated into the small motif.

Pull the dropped loop through the chain you are joining to.

Continue in the same way around the small motif. Completed assembly.

Hairpin Lace

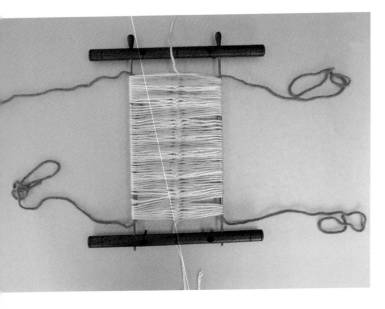

Place a slip knot on the left (first) prong. Loosen the knot until it is half the width of the space between the prongs. Reassemble the loom.

Foundation

Remove the bottom bar of the loom. Set the prongs to the required width, measuring the distance between the prongs.

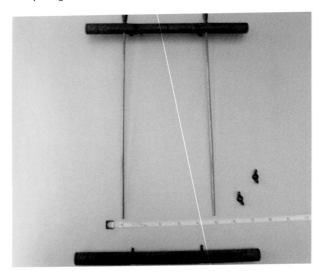

Wrap the yarn in front of the right (second) prong.

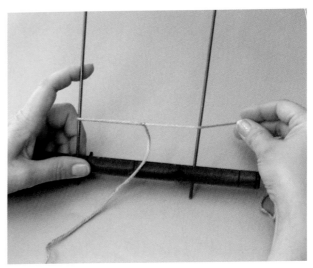

84

Continue to wrap the yarn around the back of the prongs, keeping the tension fairly tight.

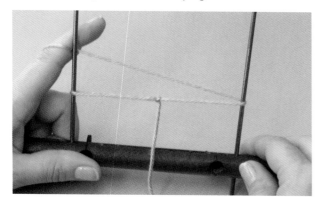

Ch 1.

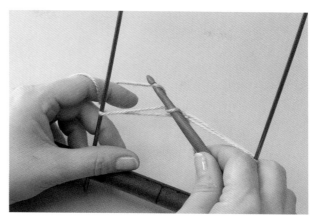

Insert the hook in the slip knot from the bottom up. Yarn over.

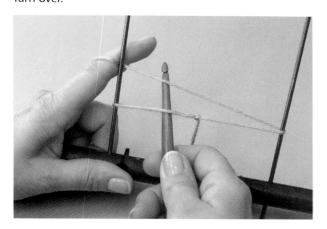

This completes your foundation.

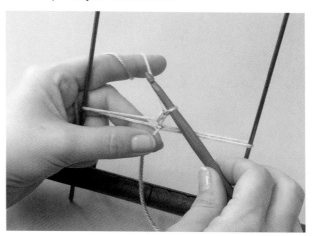

Pull the loop through the slip knot.

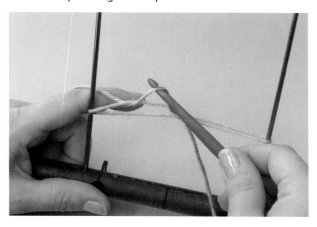

Lace Strip

Hold the loom upright in the left hand (or in the right hand for left-handed crocheters).

Step 1: Rotate the hook to point downward. Grasping the hook from behind the loom, pull the end of the hook down. Your hook is now in position for the next step.

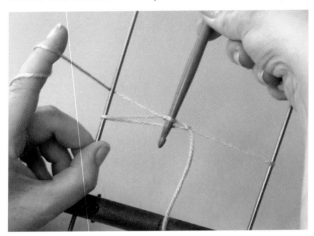

Step 2: Keeping a steady tension on the yarn, wrap it in front of the first prong, across the front of the loom, around the second prong, turning the loom clockwise until the hook is in front of the loom. The first prong should now be on the right and the second prong, on the left.

Step 3: Insert the hook from the bottom up into the loops on the left prong; yarn over and pull through.

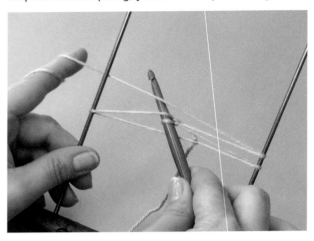

You will now have 2 loops on the hook.

Step 4: Yarn over and pull through both loops on the hook.

Hairpin Lace in the Round

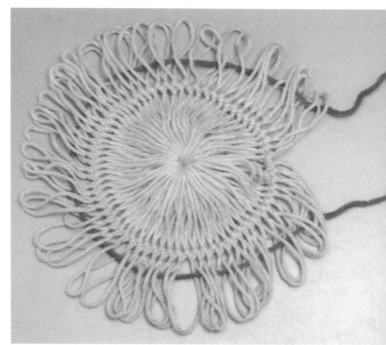

Repeat Steps 1–4 until the strip is the desired length.

Before removing the strip from the loom, use a yarn needle to draw a length of contrasting yarn through all loops on each prong.

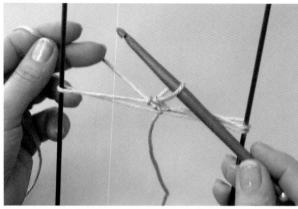

Work a hairpin lace strip in the usual manner. Remove the strip from the loom with the guide yarns in place.

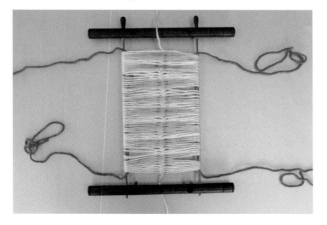

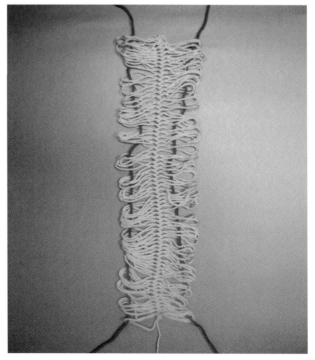

Ease the strip into a circle, bringing the top and bottom of the strip together.

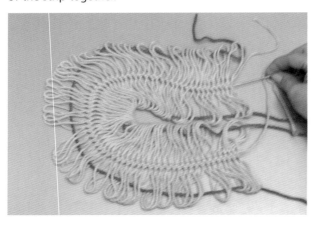

Sew the top and bottom of the strip together securely.

With a yarn needle, thread a length of matching yarn through all loops around the center, leaving a long length at each end. Remove the guide yarn from the center only.

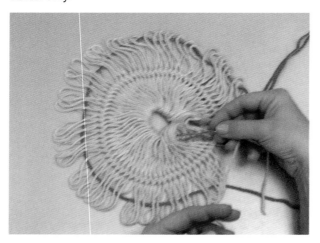

Tie the ends tightly and knot in place. Weave in loose ends.

Continue with the pattern, working in the outside loops in same manner as with regular hairpin lace and leaving the guide yarn in place until finished.

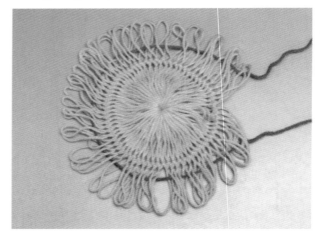

Broomstick Lace

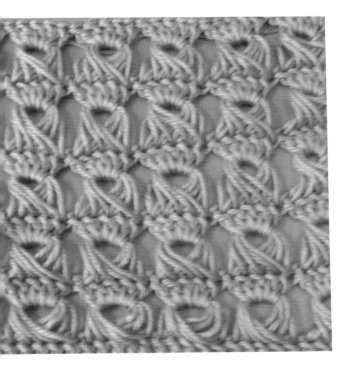

Pull the yarn through, drawing up an extra long loop.

Place the loop onto the knitting needle. Continue across until there is a loop on the knitting needle for each stitch in the row.

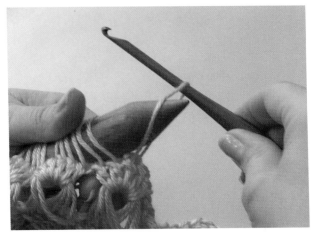

Working from left to right, insert hook in indicated stitch, yarn over.

Working from right to left, slip the hook under the number of loops indicated in the pattern.

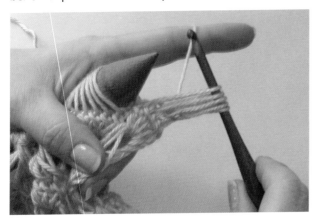

Work the indicated stitches into the group of loops.

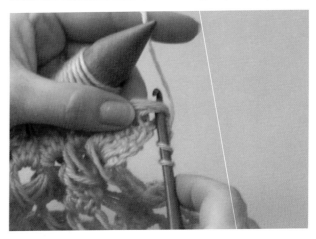

Yarn over and pull through the indicated number of loops.

Completed broomstick lace, showing 5 dc worked in each group of 5 loops.

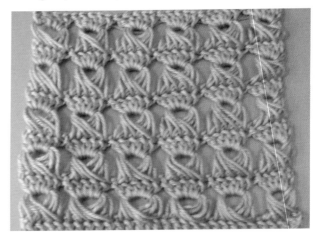

Proceed as indicated in the pattern: Ch 1 for sc, ch 2 for hdc, ch 3 for dc, or ch 4 for tr.

Broomstick Lace in the Round

For the first half of the stitches, you will work exactly the same as regular broomstick lace, placing the loops on one end of a circular knitting needle.

Insert the hook in the indicated stitch or space.

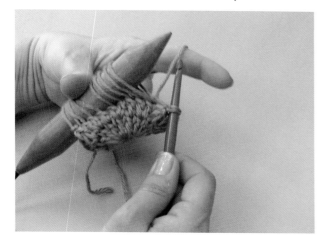

Yarn over and pull a large loop through.

Continue to pull the loop up until it is large enough, then place the loop on the knitting needle.

Once you have completed half of the stitches, you will place the remaining loops on the second end of the circular knitting needle. The two ends of the needle will be facing in opposite directions, as pictured here.

Pull up the next loop, placing it on the second end of the circular needle.

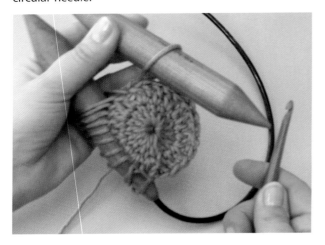

Continue placing the remaining loops on the second end of the knitting needle until all the loops have been pulled up.

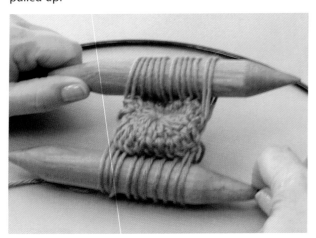

At this point, it is easiest to transfer your work to a piece of guide yarn to work the second pass. Use a yarn needle to draw a length of contrasting yarn through all the loops, then take them off the needle.

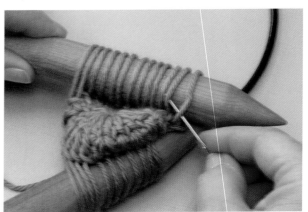

Tunisian Crochet

Each row has two stages: a forward pass and a return pass.

Forward Pass

Working from right to left, insert hook in next vertical bar.

Unlike traditional crochet, in which the stitches are worked through the two strands of yarn at the top of each stitch in the previous row, in Tunisian crochet the stitches are worked through the vertical bars on the front side of each previous row of Tunisian crochet. The vertical bars are pointed out in the photo below.

Yarn over, pull through.

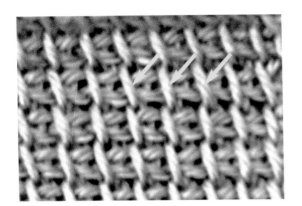

Continue across until there is one loop on the hook for each vertical bar up to last bar.

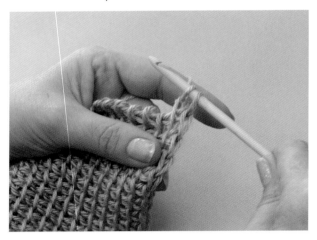

Insert hook in both the front vertical bar (as normal) and the back bar for the last stitch.

Yarn over and pull through.

All the loops remain on the hook.

Return Pass

Working from left to right, yarn over and pull through first loop on hook.

Yarn over and pull through next 2 loops on hook. Repeat until all the loops are worked off the hook.

Double-Ended Crochet

Yarn over.

Like Tunisian crochet, double-ended crochet is worked through the vertical bars in the previous row, in a forward pass and a return pass.

Forward Pass

Working with color A from right to left, insert the hook in the next vertical bar.

Pull loop through.

Repeat until there is a loop on the hook for each stitch of the previous row. Color A will now be on the left. Color B will be on the right.

Return Pass

Slide all the loops to the opposite end of the hook and turn the work. Color A will now be on the right. Color B will be on the left.

Working with color B from left to right, yarn over.

Pull through the first loop on the hook.

Yarn over.

Pull through the next 2 loops on the hook.

Both color A and color B will now be on the right end of work. To begin the next row, work the forward pass again, this time using color B to pick up loops.

This technique produces a fabric with two different—but equally attractive—sides.

Resources

Yarn

There are many wonderful yarn makers out there; these are just the ones who made the beautiful yarns featured in this book. The specific yarn or yarns used are given in italics for each manufacturer. You can find most of these yarns at your local yarn shop or craft supply store; others can be purchased online.

Bernat
Sheep(ish) by Vickie Howell
320 Livingstone Ave. South
Box 40
Listowel, ON N4W 3H3
Canada
(800) 351-8356
www.bernat.com

Berroco, Inc.
Captiva, Comfort Chunky
1 Tupperware Dr. Suite 4,
N. Smithfield, RI 02896
(401) 769-1212
www.berroco.com

Cascade Yarns
Greenland, Pure Alpaca
1224 Andover Park E.
Tukwila, WA 98188
www.cascadeyarns.com

Coats and Clark
*Aunt Lydia's Iced Bamboo,
Red Heart Boutique
Unforgettable, Red Heart
Boutique Treasure*
P.O. Box 12229
Greenville, SC 29612
(800) 648-1479
www.coatsandclark.com

Garn Studio Drops
Drops Delight
(Distributed by Nordic Mart)
www.garnstudio.com
www.nordicmart.com

Interlacements
Irish Jig, Rick Rack
3250 Froelich Rd.
Abrams, WI 54101
(920) 826-5970
www.interlacementsyarns.com

Jenny King Designs
Marigold Duke Silk
1/932 David Low Way
Marcoola QLD 4564
Austrailia
(617) 545-07077
www.jennykingdesigns.com

Knit Picks
Brava Worsted, Shine Sport
13118 NE 4th St.
Vancouver, WA 98684
(800) 574-1323
www.knitpicks.com

Kollage Yarns
Milky Whey
3591 Cahaba Beach Rd.
Birmingham, AL 35242
(888) 829-7758
www.kollageyarns.com

Lion Brand Yarn
*LB Collection Angora Merino,
LB Collection Silk Mohair*
135 Kero Rd.
Carlstadt, NJ 07072
(800) 258-9276
www.lionbrand.com

Louet North America
Euroflax
3425 Hands Rd.
Prescott, ON, Canada K0E 1T0
(800) 897-6444
www.louet.com

Tools

Jenkins Yarn Tools
*Hairpin lace loom,
circular knitting needles*
www.yarntools.com

Westing Bridge, LLC.
*Tunisian hooks, double-ended
hooks; flexible hooks*
P.O. Box 99759
Troy, MI 48083-9759
(248) 457-6887
www.chiaogoo.com

Tutorials

STITCH DIVA STUDIOS

Free online step-by-step videos for broomstick lace, hairpin lace, and Tunisian crochet, as well as online classes.

   www.stitchdiva.com

KIM GUZMAN

Free video tutorials for Tunisian crochet, plus online classes and more resources.

   www.crochetkim.com

Education

CROCHET GUILD OF AMERICA

"Think Crochet—Think CGOA!" CGOA connects amateur and professional crocheters to great resources, including the quarterly complimentary Crochet! magazine, and to local chapters, competitions, and other opportunities. The organization also hosts two yearly conferences with some of the best teachers in the industry, plus special events, contests, and opportunities for networking and socialization with other crochet enthusiasts.

   www.crochet.org

Acknowledgments

I am sure everyone has heard the old proverb, "It takes a village to raise a child." The same is true when creating a book. I am so grateful to all the people that contributed in one form or another.

All of the gorgeous yarns and tools used in this book were generously donated. I am so thankful for each and every one of you: Bernat, Berroco Inc., Cascade Yarns, Coats and Clark, Garn Studio Drops, Interlacements, Jenkins Yarn Tools, Jenny King Designs, Knit Picks, Kollage Yarns, Lion Brand Yarn, Louet North America, and Westing Bridge LLC.

Thank you also to:

Amy Shelton, for your copywriting assistance.

Angelica Soto, for your impeccable stitching of many of the models.

Brenda Bourg, for your proofreading, and cheerleading.

Chelsea Hildebrand, for your willingness to fill in for modeling.

Elizabeth Chalker, for your inspiration and support.

Gail Crooks, my second-grade teacher, for teaching me how to crochet so many years ago!

Ellen Gormley, for your wisdom and advice.

Jennifer Hansen, who taught me how to do broomstick and hairpin lace, for your influence and support in so many ways.

Kim Guzman, who has taught me so much about Tunisian and double-ended crochet, for your descriptive teaching and your willingness to always help.

Kj Hay, for being the most amazing technical editor that ever walked the earth.

Lisa Johnson, for your wonderful styling and all the laughs.

Rachel Greiser, for your styled photography and your willingness to try anything!

Sharon Silverman, for your inspiration and for opening new doors to me.

Shelby Hildebrand, for your step-by-step photography. I'm very proud of you.

Sierra Johnson, for your gorgeous modeling and for never complaining while sweltering in angora or freezing in silk.

The Crochet Guild of America, for playing such a large role in my path to success.

The "Musketeers": Vashti Braha, Doris Chan, Marty Miller, Diane Moyer. We sure have come a long way from that conference so many years ago.

I would like to thank everyone at Stackpole Books, especially Mark and Kathryn. I truly appreciate your faith in me and my vision. You have been a joy to work with.

I would also like to thank you, my readers! Without your enthusiasm for my designs I wouldn't be able to do what I do. I am very grateful for your support.

I am so thankful for my fabulous family that I sorely neglected while working on this book. Thank you for picking up my slack so I could work: George, my wonderful husband; Chelsea and Shelby, my beautiful daughters; and Willow, my perfect granddaughter. I also appreciate the support of my mother, Darlene, and my stepfather, Tony.

My greatest gratitude goes to God for this amazing talent He has given me and the opportunities He has presented in my life. I am very blessed.

Visual Index